Götz [redacted]aier-Dörner

KomplettTrainer

Englisch 7

G Gymnasium

Klett Lerntraining

Götz Maier-Dörner ist Gymnasiallehrer in Baden-Württemberg für die Fächer Englisch, Geschichte und Gemeinschaftskunde.

Aufnahmestudio: Noah-Studios, Hannover
Sprecher: Elena Bernewitz, Reading (Großbritannien); Janice Marie Morris, Hildesheim; Jonathan Haas, Hildesheim

Bibliografische Information der Deutschen Bibliothek
Die Deutsche Bibliothek verzeichnet diese Publikation in der Deutschen Nationalbibliografie; detaillierte bibliografische Daten sind im Internet über http://dnb.ddb.de abrufbar.

Auflage 4. 3. 2. 1. | 2012 2011 2010 2009
Die letzten Zahlen bezeichnen jeweils die Auflage und das Jahr des Druckes.
Dieses Werk folgt der neuesten Rechtschreibung und Zeichensetzung. Ausnahmen bilden Texte, bei denen künstlerische, philologische oder lizenzrechtliche oder andere Gründe einer Änderung entgegenstehen.

Internetadresse: www.klett.de
Zeichnungen: Naomi Fearn, Berlin: S. 9, 71, 117; Steffen Jähde, Berlin: S. 10, 15, 22, 25, 26, 34, 36, 42, 49, 50, 60, 64, 73, 76, 79, 84, 98, 110, 134, 135, 160, 167, 181
Umschlaggestaltung: Sabine Krohberger Grafikdesign, München
Umschlagfoto: Getty Images Deutschland GmbH, München
Satz: Klaus Bauer, Bondorf
Reproduktion: Meyle + Müller, Medien-Management, Pforzheim
Druck: Canale & C. S. P. A.
Printed in Europe
ISBN: 978-3-12-927101-8

9 783129 271018

Wortschatz

Englisch verstehen

Alle Tests auf einen Blick

HEY! IHR SOLLT DOCH ENGLISCH ÜBEN!!!
MOMENT, DAS IST „SCHNARRY FLOTTER“, DEN HABT IHR DOCH SCHON HUNDERT MAL GESEHEN!
...ABER DER IST JA AUF ENGLISCH! DAS HEISST, IHR LERNT WAS DABEI!!!
OK, MACHT WEITER.
SEHT IHR, ICH HAB' EUCH GESAGT ES FUNKTIONIERT!

Liebe Schülerin, lieber Schüler,

der **KomplettTrainer Englisch Gymnasium 7. Schuljahr** ist

genau das richtige Buch für dich

- weil du den **kompletten** Lernstoff mit **einem Buch** wiederholen kannst,
- weil du wichtige **Regeln und Merksätze** mit Beispielen sofort erfasst,
- weil du in vielen **Aufgaben** und **Tests** mit **ausführlichen Lösungen** das Gelernte übst und
- weil du damit gut vorbereitet in die nächste **Klassenarbeit** oder einen **Test** gehst.

So lernst du mit diesem Buch:

In der Kopfzeile siehst du 4 Rubriken: *Wissen, Übungen, Test, Checkliste.* Rot hervorgehoben ist jeweils die Rubrik, in der du dich gerade befindest.

Wissen Hier kannst du Regeln, wichtige Formeln, Merksätze und Beispiele nachschlagen.

Wissen	**Übungen**	Test	Checkliste

Übungen An vielen Übungsaufgaben in unterschiedlichen Schwierigkeitsstufen kannst du üben, üben, üben … bis du den Stoff sicher beherrscht.

Test Der Test am Ende des Kapitels zeigt dir, wie gut du bist.

Checkliste Mit der Checkliste schätzt du dich selbst ein.

Lösungen Hier kannst du sofort überprüfen, ob du die Aufgaben richtig gelöst hast oder deine Lösung korrigieren.

Die **Audio-CD** hilft dir dabei zu trainieren, gesprochene englische Texte zu verstehen. Die Hörverstehensaufgaben erkennst du im Buch am Symbol . Diese Aufgaben kannst du nur lösen, wenn du dir den zugehörigen Text auf der Audio-CD anhörst. Alle gesprochenen Texte der CD sind bei den Lösungen nochmals abgedruckt.

Viel Erfolg wünschen dir dein Autor und die Redakteure von Klett Lerntraining.

Grammatik

Hier wiederholst du

- die Bedingungssätze vom Typ I und II
- den richtigen Gebrauch von Gerundium and Infinitiv
- wann du *present perfect simple* und *progressive* verwendest
- den Unterschied zwischen *simple past* und *past progressive*
- die Bildung und Verwendung des Passiv

1 Bedingungssätze

1.1 Bedingungssätze Typ I

1 Check-up

Make sentences with the sentence machine and the information from the picture.

Susan and Max Smith are planning their holidays with their parents.

Holiday plans

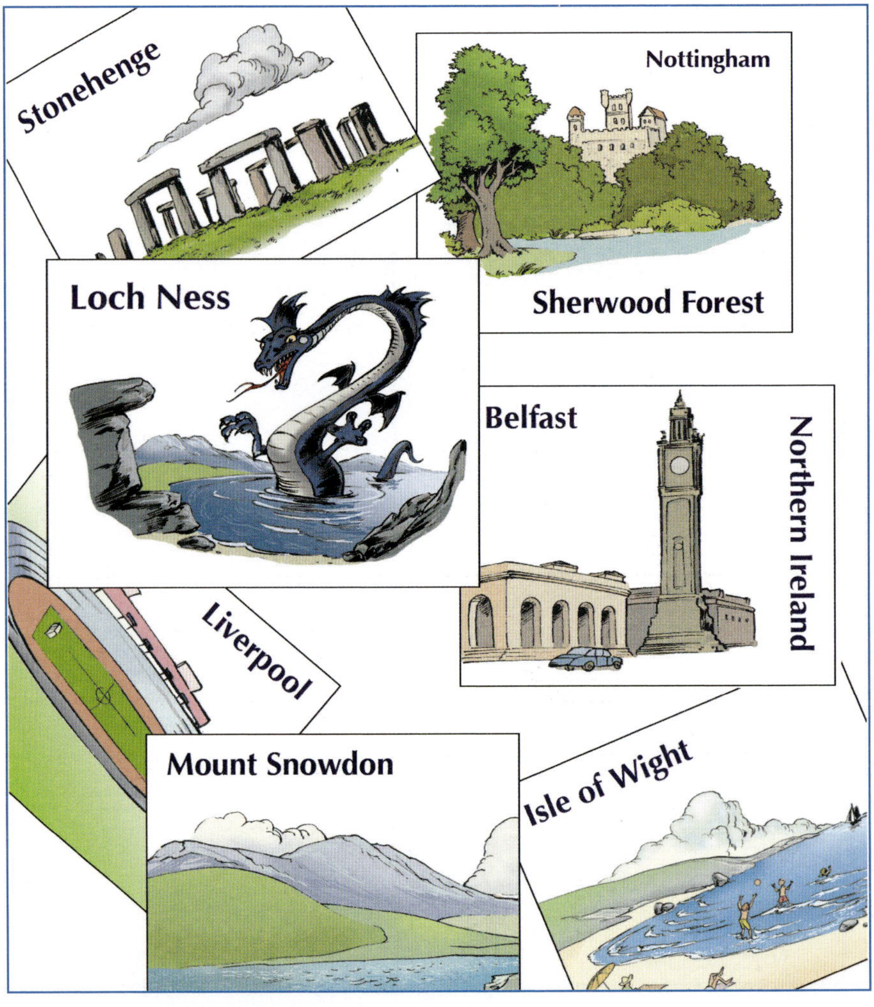

If we go to	Scotland, Liverpool, the Isle of Wight, Wales, Northern Ireland, South England, Nottingham,	I will we can we must	visit Stonehenge. spend a day at Loch Ness. take a walk in Sherwood Forest. spend a few days in Belfast. go swimming. climb Mount Snowdon. watch a football game.

1. ______________________________

____

2. ______________________________

____

3. ______________________________

____

4. ______________________________

____

5. ______________________________

____

6. ______________________________

____

7. ______________________________

____

Bedingungssätze Typ I

Wenn wir über Ereignisse reden, die nur eintreten, wenn eine bestimmte **Bedingung** erfüllt wird, verwenden wir das kleine Wörtchen **wenn**. Im Englischen ist das Wörtchen noch kleiner und heißt ***if***. Je nachdem, wie wahrscheinlich es ist, dass die Bedingung eintritt, müssen wir im Englischen die Zeiten der Verben verändern.

Bei den Sätzen im **Check-up** sind alle Vorschläge **grundsätzlich möglich** und folglich **auch wahrscheinlich**. Wir verwenden deshalb die **Bedingungssätze des Typs I.**

Bedingung (if-clause)	Folge (main clause)
If we go to Scotland, If we go to Scotland, If we go to Scotland,	I will visit Loch Ness. I won't visit Stonehenge. we can visit Edinburgh.
simple present	***will-future* oder** ***modal auxiliary + infinitive***

oder

Folge (main clause)	Bedingung (if-clause)
I will visit Stonehenge	if we go to Scotland.
will-future* oder** ***modal auxiliary + infinitive	***simple present***

Achtung: Wir setzen das Komma nur, wenn der *if*-Satz am Anfang steht!

Der Unterschied zwischen *if* und *when*

Ein typischer Fehler ist die Verwechslung von *if* und *when*.

***If* steht für Bedingungen:**
If we go to Nottingham, we will visit Sherwood Forest.

Hier ist noch nicht klar, ob sie überhaupt nach Nottingham gehen.

***When* gibt die Zeit an:**
When we are in Nottingham, I will visit Sherwood Forest.

Hier ist völlig klar, dass der Sprecher nach Nottingham geht.

2

Write sentences using *if*.

Here are some more ideas the Smiths have for their holiday.

Example:
Mr. Smith: We spend a week in Liverpool. I / watch / a football match.
"If we spend a week in Liverpool, I will watch a football match."

1. *Mrs. Smith:* Liverpool loses again. You / be / grumpy.

   ____

2. *Susan:* We / not / go swimming on the Isle of Wight. I / be / very angry.

   ____

3. *Max:* We spend time at the beach. I / build / a lot of sand castles.

   ____

4. *Mrs. Smith:* We visit Stonehenge. You / learn / a lot about history.

   ____

5. *Mr. Smith:* We climb Mount Snowdon. We / see / very far.

   ____

6. *Max:* We / not / camp at Loch Ness. I / not / see the monster.

   ____

7. *Susan:* We spend a lot of time on camping grounds. I / make / many new friends.

   ____

   ____

8. *Mrs. Smith:* We go for a walk in Sherwood Forest. I / think / of Robin Hood and his gang.

   ____

   ____

3

Turn all the sentences around so that the main clause is at the beginning of the sentence.

Example:
Mr. Smith: "I will watch a football match if we spend a week in Liverpool."

4

When or *if*? Fill in the correct word.

Here are a few things the Smiths should remember when they plan their holiday.

1. They shouldn't climb Mount Snowdon ________ they don't wear heavy boots.
2. ________ Susan wants to lie in the sun, she should use sun lotion.
3. Mrs. Smith should lock the door ________ they leave the house.
4. ________ they get into the car, they should make sure that they haven't left anything important at home.
5. They shouldn't go without a mobile phone so they can call for help ________ the car breaks down.
6. They should look for a hotel on the internet ________ they know where they want to go.
7. Mrs. Smith should take a map of Sherwood Forest ________ she wants to look for Robin Hood.
8. ________ Mr. Smith wants to see a football match, he should bring a lot of money.
9. ________ the holiday is over, they should feel relaxed.

1.2 Bedingungssätze Typ II

5 Check-up

Complete the sentences.

Of course everyone in the Smith family has dreams. Here's what they would do if they had a lot of money.

Dreams

Mrs. Smith: go on a safari

If we had a lot of money, *I would go on a safari in Africa*.

Mr. Smith: rent a VIP-lounge

If I had a lot of money, I would rent a VIP-lounge.

Susan: travel to New York

If I had a lot of money, I would travel to New York.

Max: fly to the moon

If I had a lot of money, I would fly to the moon.

Bedingungssätze Typ II

In Bedingungssätzen des Typs II wird eine Bedingung gestellt, die **sehr schwer** oder gar **unmöglich** zu erfüllen ist. Die Smiths sind nicht reich (deshalb verbringen sie ihren Urlaub auch in Großbritannien), und die Wahrscheinlichkeit, dass sie reich werden, ist äußerst gering.

Für Bedingungen, deren Erfüllung **ausgesprochen unwahrscheinlich bis unmöglich** erscheint, nehmen wir die **Bedingungssätze Typ II**.

Bedingung (if-clause)	Folge (main clause)
If he **had** a lot of money,	Max **would fly** to the moon. Max **could fly** to the moon. Max **might fly** to the moon.
simple past	***conditional I* oder *could* (könnte) oder *might* (würde vielleicht) + *infinitive***

oder

Folge (main clause)	Bedingung (if-clause)
Max **would fly** to the moon	if he **had** a lot of money.
conditional I* oder *could* (könnte) oder *might* (würde vielleicht) + *infinitive	***simple past***

Ein Sonderfall ist das deutsche „An deiner/seiner etc. Stelle würde ich …"
Hier steht im Englischen:

If I **were** you/him/her/them, I would go to Australia on holiday.

Were bleibt in allen Personen unverändert. Die Bedingung, die hier formuliert wird, ist unerfüllbar. Es handelt sich eher um eine Art Traum oder Fantasie.

6

Make sentences with the sentence machine.

Here are more dreams the Smiths have about their holidays – they're all very unlikely!

If Max	were a millionaire,	she would meet Robin Hood.
If Susan	had a plane,	he would go to the Football World Championships.
If Mrs. Smith	was old enough to drive a car,	he would drive to Loch Ness.
If Mr. Smith	was able to travel in time,	she would fly to America.

1. ______________________________

____

2. ______________________________

____

3. ______________________________

____

4. ______________________________

____

7

Find conditions and consequences that fit together and write two sentences for every family member.

Of course, crazy things can happen on a holiday. Here's what might happen and what they would then do.

Nessie / come out of the water and kiss me.	He / take me to a fancy disco.
I / take a picture of Nessie.	I / climb to the top of the Empire State Building.
I / meet a star in Manhattan.	We / invite them for dinner.
I / spend a week in Manhattan.	I / help him to kill the Sheriff of Nottingham.
I / find Robin Hood.	I / take my best friend with me.
I / kill the Sheriff of Nottingham.	I / be / a star.
I / go to the Football World Championships.	The police / arrest me.
We / meet the British team.	I / be / rich.

Max: If Nessie came out of the water and kissed me, I would be a star.

____

1. *Susan:* ______________________________

____

2. *Mrs. Smith:* ______________________________

____

3. *Mr. Smith:* ______________________________

____

8 1

Type I or II? Complete the sentences with the verb in the correct tense.

The Smiths have finally decided to go to Scotland for their holiday. Max is happy, Susan isn't.

Holidays in Scotland

Max: Isn't it great that we will spend the holidays in Scotland. If we wait long enough, we (1) __________________ (see) Nessie.

Susan: Yeah, right. And if I (2) __________________ (be) the King of China, you (3) __________________ (be) my personal Clown.

Max: Don't make fun of me, Susan. I'm sure Nessie lives down there, but you can only see it if you (4) __________________ (believe) in it.

Susan: You know, I believe in the sun, and if we go to Scotland, we (5) __________________ (not see) much of it. It always rains there.

Max: But if we (6) __________________ (go) to the Isle of Wight, we would spend all day on the beach, and that's boring after a day or two. Waiting for Nessie is much more exciting.

Susan: Oh come on, we (7) __________________ (meet) so many nice people if we went to the beach, and we (8) __________________ (lie) in the sun and relax. That's what holidays are about.

Max: But if we really go to Scotland, mom and dad (9) __________________ (show) us Edinburgh and we (10) __________________ (climb) Ben Nevis with them.

Susan: Oh forget it. If you (11) __________________ (be) as old as I am, you would understand.

1

If or *when*?

1. Max will run to the lake at once _________ the Smiths arrive at Loch Ness.
2. _________ the sun shines when they are at Loch Ness, Max will sit all day and wait for Nessie.
3. Susan will be grumpy _________ it rains at Loch Ness.
4. Loch Ness would become even more famous _________ Nessie really put her head out of the water.
5. Susan will be very happy _________ the Smiths leave Loch Ness to go to Edinburgh.
6. _________ they are at Edinburgh, she will look at the old buildings and drink a cup of coffee.

points: 6 *1 point for each gap*

2

Type I or type II? Tick the correct box.

	Type I	Type II
If Mrs. Smith finds a job soon, the Smiths will go to America next year.	☐	☐
Susan would be very excited if they went there.	☐	☐
Max said: "I will only go if there are monsters in America."	☐	☐
Then Susan said: "If we found a monster, it would probably be King Kong."	☐	☐
If they go there, Mrs. Smith will read a lot of books about American history.	☐	☐

points: 5 *1 point for each box*

3

Complete the sentences by translating the German phrases.

After the holidays

1. *Susan:* If we go to Scotland again next year, ______________________ ______________________ **(bleibe ich zu Hause)**.
2. *Mr. Smith:* We will only go on holiday next year, ______________________ ______________________ **(wenn wir genug Geld haben)**.
3. *Max:* If we took part in the lottery, ______________________ ______________________ **(könnten wir viel Geld gewinnen)**.
4. *Susan:* Yes, and we would all be happier ______________________ ______________________ **(wenn du ruhig wärest)**.
5. *Mrs. Smith:* Right, and your brother would be a much happier child ______________________ **(wenn er eine nette Schwester hätte)**.
6. *Mr. Smith:* "That's right, but maybe Susan can go to a camp next year ______________________ **(falls wir nach Schottland fahren)**.
7. *Max:* Yes, that's a good idea. If she isn't there, ______________________ ______________________ **(wird Nessie kommen und mich küssen)**.

2 points for each sentence points: ___ /14

0–12 points ☹	12–19 points 😐	20–25 points ☺
Too many mistakes – read this chapter again!	That was OK, but you can do better!	You did a really good job!

maximum number of points: ___ /25

2 Gerundium und Infinitiv

2.1 Das Gerundium

1 Check-up

What are their jobs? Find the correct job from the description below and write it in the gap. Of course, only three are right.

teacher **bus driver** **doctor**

vet **nurse** **manager**

I love my job because I enjoy working with animals. I also think that making the owners happy is great.	I hate driving all day and arguing with people who don't have a ticket. I would prefer working on a farm.	I love making a lot of money and working all the time. I hate sitting at home doing nothing. Meeting important people is also great.
He's a ____________.	He's a ____________.	She's a ____________.

Das Gerundium

Ein Gerundium (*gerund)* ist eigentlich nur ein **Verb in der -ing-Form**, das fast genauso verwendet wird wie ein Substantiv. Sieh dir den folgenden Beispielsatz aus dem Check-up noch einmal an:

S	V	O		
I	hate	sitting	at home doing nothing.	*Man könnte auch sagen:*
I	hate	bad food.		

Im zweiten Satz ist *bad food* das Objekt, im Satz aus dem Check-up ist es *sitting:* das *gerund* steht hier also anstelle eines Substantivs.
Das *gerund* kann im Englischen in verschiedenen Funktionen auftreten, z. B. auch als Subjekt des Satzes, und wird oft verwendet, um zu sagen, ob man etwas mag, nicht mag, ob einen etwas interessiert oder ob man etwas gut oder nicht so gut kann.

Das *gerund* als Subjekt

Singing is terrible.
Playing football can be great.

Das *gerund* als Objekt

I hate **singing**.
I love **playing football**.

Das *gerund* nach Adjektiven mit Präpositionen

He is bad at **singing**.
I'm good at **playing football**.

2 2

Find the clauses and sentences that have a gerund and underline them. Then put them into the correct column in the table.

At school today, Andrea's class is having a discussion about hobbies.

Hobbies

Alice: I love meeting friends. That's the best, because you can talk and have fun.

Andrew: That's right, especially if they like doing the same things as I do.

Fiona: I agree, but I think reading is great, too, because I can do that at home in my room when I'm alone.

Alex: Bah, I'm tired of reading. We have to read at school all the time. I'm good at doing sports and I'm excellent at playing football. Those are my hobbies.

Tim: I think doing sports is OK, but I'm terrible at playing football. I prefer skiing, it's a lot of fun and I'm good at it.

Sarah: I think that going shopping is also a great hobby. I love looking at new books and clothes in the shops. I only wish I had more money.

Kirk: I disagree, shopping is terrible. Listening to music is so much more fun. I'm also interested in finding out about pop and rock groups, so I also enjoy reading magazines about the music scene.

Gerund used as subject	Gerund used as object	Gerund used after adjective + preposition
	I love meeting friends	

3

Gerunds as objects. Finish the sentences.

Here are other members of the class. What do or don't they like doing?

What do or don't they like doing?

Mary: 	John: 	Alice: 
Sarah: 	Abdul: 	Philip: 

Example: *Mary likes singing.*

1. John loves ________________________________.
2. Alice enjoys ________________________________.
3. Sarah hates ________________________________.
4. Abdul doesn't like ________________________________.
5. Philip likes ________________________________.

4

Gerunds as subjects. Write sentences using words from the boxes.

During the break, the teachers also talk about their hobbies, and the things they don't enjoy doing.

What teachers like or don't like doing

Example: *Mr. Bond: Playing with children is not much fun.*

Mr. Hunt: ______________________________

Mrs. Giggs: ______________________________

Mr. Miller: ______________________________

Mrs. Hathaway: ______________________________

Mr. Singh: ______________________________

Mrs. Bangs: ______________________________

Mr. Smith: ______________________________

Mrs. Sander: ______________________________

5 3

Gerund after adjectives and prepositions. Complete the sentences using words from the boxes. Of course the words from the left box can be used more than once.

After the discussion about hobbies, the pupils talk about their families.

good at terrible at interested in not very good at tired of	run teach French keep things in order do sports teach Maths cook play chess

Alice: My dad is a doctor. *He's very good at helping ill people.*

Philip: My dad is very chaotic. So he is ______________________________________.

Hilary: My mother is a French teacher. She is ______________________ ______________________ but I'm sure she would be ______________________.

Alex: My brother is so slow. So he is ______________________ but he is ______________________.

Sarah: You know, my little sister is really ______________________. That's why she got five cook books for her birthday.

Abdul: My brother is just as ______________________ as I am. He says it makes him hot, thirsty and tired. Sports are terrible.

2.2 Der Infinitiv

6 Check-up

Use the words given below to build correct sentences.

1. to listen / doesn't allow me / My mother / to loud music

   ____

2. tells me / to go to bed / early / She always

   ____

3. when the weather is nice / to do homework / It's really difficult

   ____

4. to tell children what to do / I think / it's wrong

   ____

5. hates / to be strict with me / My mother

   ____

Der Infinitiv

Ebenso wie das Gerundium steht der **Infinitiv** nach bestimmten Verben oder Adjektiven. Da beide im Satz oft ähnliche Funktionen erfüllen, ist es wichtig zu wissen, in welchen Fällen man den **Infinitv** nimmt, in welchen das **Gerundium** und in welchen beides möglich ist.
Wir beschränken uns hier nur auf Fälle, in denen der **Infinitiv** mit *to* steht.

1. Der **Infinitiv** steht nach bestimmten Verben und deren Objekt.

   I asked him **to help** me.
   She teaches me **to play** football.
   The teacher ordered him **to leave** the room.

   Genauso funktionieren: to allow, to tell

2. Außerdem steht der **Infinitiv** nach folgenden Adjektiven:

It's easy **to do** your homework early in the afternoon.
It was wrong **not to learn** for the last class test.

Genauso funktionieren: difficult, hard, right

3. Nach manchen Verben kann man sowohl ein **Gerund** als auch einen **Infinitiv** verwenden, ohne dass sich die Bedeutung verändert.

He began **to learn / learning** for the test last week.
I hate **to get / getting** bad marks on tests.

Genauso funktionieren: to continue, to love, to like, to start, to prefer

4. **Vorsicht bei *stop, remember, forget*!** Hier verändert sich die Bedeutung, je nachdem ob du einen Infinitiv oder ein Gerundium verwendest.

When we met Alice in town yesterday, we stopped **to talk** to her.	Als wir Alice gestern in der Stadt trafen, hielten wir an, um mit ihr zu sprechen. **anhalten, um etwas zu tun**
I stopped **eating** lunch.	Ich beendete das Mitagessen. **mit etwas aufhören**

Please don't forget (remember) **to come** to my birthday party this year.	Bitte vergiss nicht (denke daran), dieses Jahr zu meiner Geburtstagsparty zu kommen. **daran denken, etwas zu tun**
I remember (didn't forget) **coming** to your party two years ago.	Ich erinnere mich (habe nicht vergessen), dass ich vor zwei Jahren auf deiner Party war. **sich daran erinnern / nicht vergessen haben, etwas getan zu haben**

7

Make 14 sentences using an infinitive. Use all the phrases from the column on the right.

Hobbies are great, duties* can be terrible

My parents Our teachers My friends	always often never sometimes	ask me order me allow me tell me	to clean up my room. to do my homework. to help them with their homework. to leave the room. to stay out late in the evening. to go to parties. work in the garden. to clean up the playground.
I think I'm sure I believe I don't think	it's difficult it's not right it's easy it's hard	to be a pop star. to order pupils to clean the playground. to earn a lot of money. to hit your friends. to be nice to somebody I don't like. to tell teenagers when to be home in the evening.	

***duty** – Pflicht

8

Gerund, infinitive or both? Mark the correct sentence. Of course, sometimes both are correct.

1. Cleaning the house is great. ☒
   To clean the house is great. ☐
2. I hate to do extra work for school. ☐
   I hate doing extra work for school. ☐
3. My father is excellent at cooking. ☐
   My father is excellent at to cook. ☐

4. Yesterday my class began to do a new project on hobbies. ☐
   Yesterday my class began doing a new project on hobbies. ☐

5. My friends and I believe it's wrong to send teenagers to school. ☐
   My friends and I believe it's wrong sending teenagers to school. ☐

6. I really love to do homework. ☐
   I really love doing homework. ☐

7. I hope my parents will allow me to buy a new CD tomorrow. ☐
   I hope my parents will allow me buying a new CD tomorrow. ☐

8. If I continue getting good marks, my parents will buy me a present. ☐
   If I continue to get good marks, my parents will buy me a present. ☐

9. My best friend really enjoys to eat a lot. ☐
   My best friend really enjoys eating a lot. ☐

9

Mark the correct translation.

1. *Ich bin sicher, dass er nicht vergessen wird dich anzurufen.*
   I'm sure he won't forget to phone you. ☐
   I'm sure he won't forget phoning you. ☐

2. *Ich habe vergessen, dass ich das Buch gekauft habe.*
   I didn't remember to buy the book. ☐
   I didn't remember buying the book. ☐

3. *Ich werde sicherlich daran denken, dir eine Postkarte zu schicken.*
   I'm sure I will remember sending you a postcard. ☐
   I'm sure I will remember to send you a postcard. ☐

4. *Der Fahrer des Wagens hielt an, um aus dem Fenster zu schauen.*
   The driver of the car stopped looking out of the window. ☐
   The driver of the car stopped to look out of the window. ☐

1

Find the mistakes and correct them. Be careful: two sentences are correct as they are.

1. Yesterday my girlfriend asked me doing her homework on the bus.

   ____

2. It was really early in the morning and I'm terrible at doing homework so early.

   ____

3. So I said: "To do homework on the bus is not right. You should do it at home."

   ____

4. She answered: "Stop to say such stupid things and help me!"

   ____

5. I told her leaving me alone and closed my eyes.

   ____

6. She started screaming at me and walked away.

   ____

7. Now I'm looking for a new girlfriend and I will make sure that she prefers to do her homework at home.

   ____

points: 7   *1 point for each sentence*

2

Underline all the infinitives and the words that make them necessary in one colour, and do the same with the gerunds in a different colour.

Hobbies and free time

Most teenagers love having as much free time as possible. They find it easy to spend day after day at home with their friends or they go outside and do sports or walk around town. Most of them hate doing homework although some like to do it, too. Often teenagers must ask their parents to allow them to go somewhere, especially in the evenings. Many parents find it difficult to say "no" when that happens, but they of course say it anyway. Most teenagers are terrible at accepting a "no" from their parents, and they start to argue with them. Usually, they both – teenagers and parents – hate having these discussions, and usually the parents win. But still, teenagers continue to fight for their freedom* and will never stop doing so. Growing up is a difficult time, but many parents would say that being a parent is almost as difficult, too.

***freedom** – Freiheit

1 point for each gerund or infinitive points: ___ 14

3

Three infinitives can be replaced by a gerund and three gerunds can be replaced by an infinitive. Find and replace them.

1. ______
2. ______
3. ______
4. ______
5. ______
6. ______

1 point for each replacement points: ___ 6

0–13 points ☹	14–21 points 😐	22–27 points ☺
Too many mistakes – read this chapter again!	That was OK, but you can do better!	You did a really good job!

maximum number of points: ___ 27

3 Das *present perfect simple* und *progressive*

1 Check-up

Complete the sentences with the present perfect.

It's Sunday morning. Andrew and Alice have given a party. It has just ended. Their parents are away for the weekend. In the picture you can see what the living room looks like after the party.

Example: A "very funny" guest has broken **(to break)** a lot of glasses.

1. Some guests ______________________ **(to watch)** TV.
2. People ______________________ **(to eat)** a lot of crisps.
3. An idiot ______________________ **(to paint)** a red heart on the mirror.
4. The CD-player ______________________ **(to fall)** off the sideboard.
5. Many people ______________________ **(to leave)** their empty bottles on the floor.

2 Check-up 4

Complete the sentences with verbs in the present perfect progressive.

Luckily, their parents are home an hour late, so Andrew and Alice have been able to clean up the house in time. Alice and Andrew hear the car coming, and meet their parents when they're getting out of the car.

Mr. Smith: Oh hi. It's great to be home. Our trip was terrible. Look at the weather. It has been raining (to rain) all day and we ______________________ (1) (to drive) for hours.

Mrs. Smith: Yes, it was awful, but I didn't mind because I was asleep until a minute ago. What __________ you __________ __________________ (2) (to do) all morning?

Andrew: Oh … well … err … … hm …

Alice: We ______________________ (3) (to watch) TV. There is a great show on. Do you want to watch with us?

Das *present perfect simple* und das *present perfect progressive*

Das *present perfect* hat – anders als das *past tense* – immer einen klaren **Bezug zur Gegenwart**. Betrachten wir einige Sätze aus dem Check-up.

Present perfect simple	Present perfect progressive
Many people **have left** their bottles on the floor.	We **have been watching** TV.
Die Handlung wurde in der Vergangenheit abgeschlossen (oft erst in diesem Moment), ihr Ergebnis ist aber in der Gegenwart sichtbar (Die Flaschen liegen noch da.) oder ist für die Gegenwart bedeutend. (Die Flaschen müssen aufgeräumt werden.)	Betont wird, dass die Handlung in der Vergangenheit begann, bis in die Gegenwart fortdauerte und möglicherweise sogar noch **in der Zukunft** weitergehen wird.

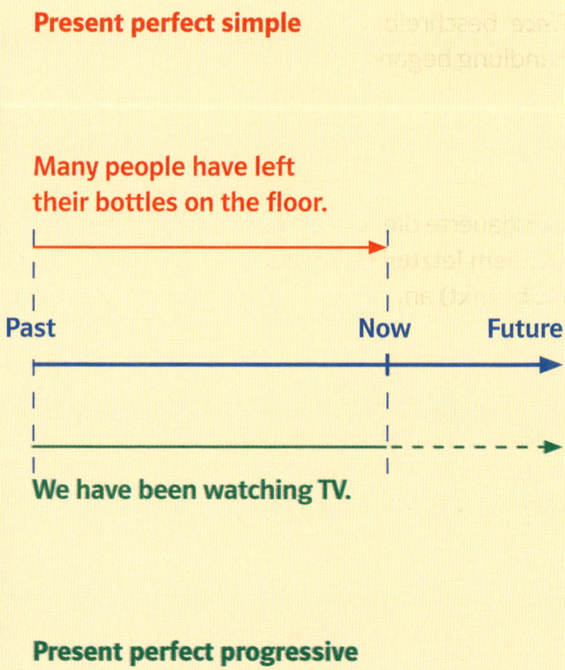

For und *since*

Sowohl das *present perfect simple* als auch das *present perfect progressive* haben ***for*** und ***since*** als Signalwörter. Da wir beide im Deutschen mit **seit** übersetzen, ist es wichtig, den Unterschied im Englischen zu kennen.

For beschreibt einen **längeren Zeitraum**.

I haven't danced **for two months**.

Zwei Monate (längerer Zeitraum) hat die Person nicht getanzt. Ob sie heute tanzen wird, wissen wir nicht.

We've been dancing **for hours**.

Wir wissen nicht, wann diese Leute das letzte Mal getanzt haben. Wichtig ist, dass sie **seit Stunden (längerer Zeitraum)** tanzen und möglicherweise noch weitertanzen werden.

Since beschreibt den **Zeitpunkt in der Vergangenheit,** an dem eine Handlung begann.

I haven't eaten so many crisps **since my last birthday**.

Hier dauerte die „chipsfreie" Zeit **seit dem letzten Geburtstag (Zeitpunkt)** an.

I've been eating crisps **since I came here**. They are so great.

Hier wird wieder nur Wert darauf gelegt, dass **seit der Ankunft (Zeitpunkt)** Chips gegessen wurden und wohl noch weiter gegessen werden.

Weitere Signalwörter für das *present perfect simple* sind ***ever, never, just, already, yet.***

3.1 Irregular verbs

Wenn du das *present perfect* richtig verwenden möchtest, musst du die unregelmäßigen Verben kennen. Hier hast du die Chance, einige von ihnen zu wiederholen.

3

Here is a chain of irregular verbs in the infinitive: find the verbs and draw a line between them. Be careful! One verb is regular!

ringwritelearnseedrinkshowbereadleavecuthearfeelcomemeeteat

4

Find out which of the verbs from exercise 3 fits in which sentence, and write the past participle (third form) of the verb into the crossword puzzle.

Party Talk I

1. "Oh, my parents have just **(4 across)** an email. They will be home tonight!" – "Wow, I think we should start cleaning up then."
2. "Have you **(3 down)** your vocabulary for tomorrow's test yet?" – "No, I played football all afternoon."
3. "Wow, Ally has **(1 down)** Melissa's hair." – "Well, I don't think that was a good idea."

4. "Have you already **(7 down)** the pictures from Australia? Andrea has just **(7 across)** them to me. They are great." – "No, I haven't. Have you ever **(6 down)** to Australia?" – "No, I haven't, but I have **(13 down)** a lot of books about it."
5. "Oh my glass is empty. Who has **(2 down)** my coke?" – "I don't know, just get a new one!"
6. "Where's Jane? Has she already **(14 across)**?" – "Yes, she left an hour ago."
7. "Look Alice, the boy over there … the one who has just **(5 down)** in. Have you **(11 across)** of him? He's the new boy from Birmingham. Isn't he cute?"
8. "Hi Maria, this is my friend Gabriele." – "Oh I know, we have just **(8 down)**."
9. "Andrew, the doorbell has just **(12 down)**. Could you please go and open the door?" – "No, do it yourself. Can't you see that I'm dancing?"
10. "Oh my goodness. I will never move again. I have **(10 across)** too many crisps. I have never **(9 down)** as stuffed in my whole life."

3.2 Das *present perfect simple*

5 (CD) 5

Choose the correct verb and complete the sentences using the simple present perfect. You can listen to the CD to check your answers.

not see	turn	meet *(2x)*	break up *(Schluss machen)*
(not) bring	buy	write	

Talk before the party

Mary and Kate are getting ready for the party.

Mary: This will be a great evening, and Pete will be there, too.

have ________ you ever ________ (1) him?

Kate: No, I haven't. But we ________________ (2) emails to each other.

Mary: Oh really? That's nice. Do you know how old he is?

Kate: I think he ________ just ________ (3) sixteen. His birthday was a week ago.

Mary: That's old. I thought he was younger. What about Billy?

I ________________ (4) him for weeks.

Kate: I met him last week. I think he will be there, but his girlfriend ________ just ________________ (5) with him. I think her name was Donna.

Mary: Oh, that's good news. Now he's free again and he's only fourteen. That's a better age for us, isn't it? ________ you ________ (6) that new make-up? I think we should use it today.

Kate: Oh no, it's not in my bag. I ________________________ (7) it. Well, maybe he'll like us anyway.

Mary: That's terrible, Kate! Why do you always forget important things?

I ________ never ________ (8) anyone like you.

3.3 Das *present perfect progressive*

6 (CD) 6

Choose the correct verb and complete the sentences using the present perfect progressive. You can listen to the CD to check your answers.

(not) shine	**dance *(2x)***	**sit**
go out *(miteinander gehen)*	**talk**	

Party talk II

Kate: Wow, Alice, what a great party – and so many people!

Alice: Thank you Kate. We're very, very happy. The music is great, so people have been dancing (1) since the beginning.

Mary: How about Billy? Is he here?

Alice: Yes he is. He has been sitting (2) over there for two hours. I don't think he's very happy.

Kate: I'm not surprised. His girlfriend has just broken up with him. They have been going out (3) for two months.

Mary: That's a long time. I would be sad, too. Oh, hi Pete.

Pete: Hi, what have you been talking (4) about?

Kate: Oh, umm, the weather. Nice, isn't it?

Pete: Yes, the sun hasn't been shining (5) for weeks now. Would you like to go outside anyway? I have been dancing (6) for an hour. I need some fresh air.

Kate: Umm, of course. See you later, Mary.

3.4 *Present perfect simple* oder *progressive*?

7

Use the verbs and the information from the pictures to build sentences in the present perfect simple or progressive.

Scenes from the party

Example:

to dance / since 9:00 p.m.

1.

to kiss / for 10 minutes

2.

to eat / pizza

3.

to talk / since the party started

4.

to paint / a heart on the mirror

5.

to fall asleep / just

6.

to meet / just

7.

to stand in line / for half an hour

Example: *They've been dancing since 9:00 p.m.*

3.5 *For* oder *since*?

8 7

Complete the sentences with *for* or *since*. Remember: a point in time or a period of time? You can listen to the CD to check your answers.

Talk after the party

Sarah: Have you heard that Pete is moving away to London?

Alice: Yes I have, and he has only lived here ________ (1) two years.

Sarah: That's right. I'm very sad, and Kate will be very sad, too. She has only been going out with him ________ (2) yesterday's party.

Alice: I know, how terrible. You know, she has been in love with him ________ (3) years. But did you see Steve and Maria shouting at each other? I think they broke up yesterday.

Sarah: No, I don't think so. They've been shouting at each other ________ (4) they started going out.

Alice: I think you're right, and they've been going out ________ (5) a long time.

Sarah: Yes, at least for four weeks. I don't think I could go out with a boy for more than two weeks. I've been going out with Andrew ________ (6) last Sunday and he is *so* boring.

Alice: I agree, but I've been alone ________ (7) three weeks now and that's boring, too.

Sarah: You know, life is terrible and boys are, too.

1

Write down what they have and haven't done yet.

It's the morning before the party. Here's Alice's and Andrew's to do list.

- *write and send out invitations*	*yes*
- *buy soft drinks*	*yes*
- *put up posters*	*no*
- *make food*	*yes*
- *ask friends for help*	*no*

Preparing a party

1. They have Wrote and send out invitations.
2. They have bought soft drink.
3.
4.
5.

points: 5 *1 point for each sentence*

2

Write down what the people said.

When they call their friends, they are all busy, so they can't answer the phone. When they have finished what they were doing, they call back and explain what they have been doing.
Write their statements in the present perfect progressive!

1. Maria: talk to Billy – *I have* .
2. Kate: buy new make-up –
3. Steve: shout at Maria –
4. Maria: scream at Steve –
5. Billy: think of his girlfriend –

points: 5 *1 point for each sentence*

3 8

Choose the correct verb from the box and complete the sentences, using *for* or *since* where necessary. But be careful: three verbs are not used at all. Choose the simple or progressive tense.

buy – talk – (not) work – think – wake up
make – (not) eat – (not) do – wait – dance

Giving a party is not always fun!

Alice: Andrew, could you please get up and help me? You **(1)** ____________ ____________ anything **(2)** ____________ three hours and the party starts in half an hour.

Andrew: That's not true. I **(3)** ____________ about all the things that we must still do. It's terrible, I **(4)** ____________ so much in years.

Alice: Very funny, Andrew. I **(5)** ____________ all the food, look! Could you please carry it to the living-room?

Andrew: "OK. Oh, Alice, **(6)** ________ you ________ the soft drinks yet?

Alice: You bought the soft drinks yesterday, remember? You are such an idiot, Andrew.

Andrew: Right, I remember. I think I start to forget things because I **(7)** ____________ anything **(8)** ____________ breakfast.

Alice: Don't touch the food, Andrew. I **(9)** ____________ ____________ for this party **(10)** ________ three weeks now, and I want to be perfect!

Andrew: You are so boring, little sister!

1 point for each gap — *points:* ___ / 10

0–10 points ☹	11–15 points 😐	16–20 points ☺
Too many mistakes – read this chapter again!	That was OK, but you can do better!	You did a really good job!

maximum number of points: 20

4 Das *simple past* und das *past progressive*

1 Check-up

Make sentences using the machine.

Getting ready for a class trip to London

While	Philip Maria and Sarah	were shopping food for the flight, was closing his suitcase, were driving to the airport, was leaving the house,	the zipper* broke. their car broke down. Maria lost her wallet. he lost his mobile phone.

***zipper** – Reißverschluss

1. ______________________________

____

2. ______________________________

____

3. ______________________________

____

4. ______________________________

____

Das *past progressive* und das *simple past*

Genauso wie das *present progressive* wird **das *past progressive*** für Handlungen verwendet, die längere Zeit benötigen – nur eben in der Vergangenheit.

We **were eating** lunch between 1 o'clock and 2 o'clock yesterday.

Das ***simple past*** wird verwendet, um über Dinge zu sprechen, die in der Vergangenheit abgeschlossen wurden – z. B. auch wenn man eine Geschichte erzählt.

First we **ate** lunch, then we **went** to the British Museum.

Das *past progressive* kommt selten alleine vor. Meistens wird es verwendet, um eine länger andauernde Handlung in der Vergangenheit zu beschreiben, während der eine andere Handlung einsetzt. Diese zweite Handlung steht dann im *simple past*. Um dies zu verdeutlichen, beinhalten die Sätze oft ***while*** oder ***when***. Im Wesentlichen gibt es die folgenden beiden Satzmuster:

NS	HS
While we **were visiting** the British Museum,	somebody **stole** a painting.

Das *past progressive* steht im Nebensatz mit *while* (während), im Hauptsatz steht das *simple past*.

HS	NS
We **were eating** lunch	**when** the rain **stopped**.

Das *past progressive* steht im Hauptsatz, im Nebensatz steht das *simple past* mit *when (als)*.

4.1 Das *simple past*

2

Write sentences in the simple past.

Philip's class went on a trip to London. During the trip he took notes so he could write an article for the class diary.

Philip's notes

1. board / the plane / we / at 7 a.m.

   ____

2. be / very early / this

   ____

3. the flight / OK / be

   ____

4. go / to the youth hostel / we / first / in London

   ____

5. everybody / at the youth hostel / to their rooms / go

   ____

   ____

6. take / after that / a sightseeing tour / we

   ____

   ____

7. the tour / during / become / sick / Mr. Hunt

   ____

   ____

8. we / in the evening / supper / have / at an Indian restaurant

   ____

   ____

4.2 Das *past progressive*

3

Complete the sentences. Use the past progressive.

Back home Philip adds some pictures, and describes what people were doing.

1.

The plane arrived on time but Andy and Tom ______________________ ______________________ **(sleep)** at the airport.

2.

What did Alice do during the flight? Of course she ______________________ ______________________ **(look)** out of the window the whole time.

3.

All the way to the youth hostel, Maria ______________________ **(talk)** to Mr. Hunt.

4.

In the evening we ______________________ ______________ **(have)** a great supper but Mr. Hunt ______________________ **(sleep)** at the youth hostel.

4.3 *Simple past* und *past progressive* in Sätzen mit *when* und *while*

4

Write sentences with the simple past and the past progressive. Use *when* and *while*. Use the same structure as in the example.

The next day at 3 o'clock in the afternoon there was a terrible thunderstorm in London. That evening the class and Mr. Hunt talk about what they were doing when it started to rain.

Thunderstorm in London

Example:

get up

1.

sit / in Hyde Park

2.

visit / British Museum

3.

walk through / Madame Tussaud's

4.

enter / Harrod's

5.

look at / elephants

Example: *I was getting up when it started to rain.*
or: While I was getting up, it started to rain.

1. We ____.

   While ____.

2. ____

   ____

3. ____

   ____

4. ____

   ____

5. ____

   ____

5

Complete the sentences with the verbs in the correct tense: simple past or past progressive?

A lot of other things happened to the pupils on their trip.

Example:
Philip: We *were walking* **(walk)** across Trafalgar Square when suddenly Hugh Grant *stepped* **(step)** out of a car.

Things happening in London

1. *Andrea:* That's nothing! We ____________________ **(see)** an elephant walk into Harrod's while we ____________________ **(sit)** across the street in a snack bar.
2. *Sarah:* Oh did you? Well, the police ____________________ **(arrest)** me while I ____________________ **(look)** at CDs in a shop. They thought I wanted to steal them.

3. *Archie:* That's terrible. But I saw something much more terrible. A lady ______________________ **(lie)** in the middle of the street when I ______________________ **(come)** around a corner. She was hurt, so I called an ambulance, of course.

4. *Jessica:* At Speaker's Corner a lot of people ______________________ **(talk)** at the same time when I ______________________ **(arrive)** and I couldn't understand a word so I decided to leave again. While I ______________________ **(leave)**, though, suddenly everybody ______________________ **(start)** screaming. I turned around and saw a horse running into all the people. It was very frightening. Luckily nobody was hurt.

5. *Alice:* We ______________________ **(watch)** a play at the theatre when suddenly the fire alarm ______________________ **(go)** off. It was very strange, and while everybody ______________________ **(run)** to the emergency exits, one of the actors ______________________ **(say)**: "Hey, please stay here, the alarm is part of our play." That was very funny.

6. *Khavita:* While we ______________________ **(eat)** lunch at a snack bar, a spider ______________________ **(fall)** into my soup. When I finally ______________________ **(stop)** screaming, everybody ______________________ **(look)** at me.

7. *David:* Aren't big cities crazy? At home in Kansas nothing exciting ever happens. The strangest thing that has happened to me there was that the electricity ______________________ **(go)** off while I ______________________ **(watch)** TV.

6

Complete the sentences using *when* or *while*.

Andrea writes an article for the diary, too. She writes about the museum that shows the Great Fire of London.

London, 10/7/06

On Tuesday after breakfast we visited a museum that shows a model of the Great Fire of London. In September 1666 a baker forgot to put out the fire in his oven ___________ he went to bed. ___________ he was sleeping, the fire got out of control and his house started burning. ___________ he woke up he immediately left the house to call for help. ___________ people were coming for help, he was already trying to put out the fire, but he could see that it was too late. A strong wind that night made everything worse. ___________ the firefighters were trying to save one house, another would start burning because the wind was blowing the fire everywhere. ___________ the sun came up the next morning, everybody in London was fighting the flames but the fire went on burning for five days. ___________ the people realized that water was not enough to stop the fire, they destroyed houses and even used gunpowder. Fortunately*, only six people died ___________ the fire was burning. That was of course very lucky. After the fire the people started to clean up, and ___________ they were doing this, an architect named Christopher Wren was already making plans to rebuild London. This time he used mostly stone, not wood, to build the houses.
I think this was a great museum because the model showed how the fires became bigger and bigger. ___________ we were watching it, a lady told us many interesting stories about what happened during the fire.

***fortunately** – glücklicherweise

1

Write sentences using *when* or *while*.

1. John look at Big Ben / bells start to toll*

   ____

   when ______________________________.

2. Sarah look at Buckingham Palace / the Queen look out of the window

   ____

   when suddenly ______________________________.

3. Laura and Ben visit London Zoo / an ape break out of its cage

   While ______________________________

   ______________________________.

4. Mr. Hunt shop at a flea market / a thief steal his wallet

   While ______________________________

   ______________________________.

5. Alice and Mary stand in a queue in front of Madame Tussaud's / they become hungry

   ____

   when ______________________________.

***to toll** – läuten

points: 5 *1 point for each sentence*

2

Complete the sentences using verbs in the correct tense.

Mary writes about Mr. Hunt's terrible class trip to London.

Poor Mr. Hunt, he really had a terrible trip to London. When we ______________ (get) on the plane, we almost forgot Andy and Lisa because they ______________ (sleep) in the departure lounge*. Then on the plane there was no food for him. All the pupils ______________ (enjoy) their meals when the stewardess ______________ (see) that they didn't have enough food for everybody. Well, I gave him a bite of my sandwich at least. Later at the youth hostel he became ill. The first three days we were looking at all the sights while poor Mr. Hunt ______________ (lie) in bed. When he was finally healthy again, other terrible things happened: While he ______________ (wait) in the queue at the British Museum, it ______________ (start) to rain and he ______________ (get) wet. Then someone ______________ (steal) his wallet while he ______________ (shop) at a flea market. It was a terrible trip for him – but we loved it.

***departure lounge** – Warteraum auf dem Flugplatz

1 point for each gap points: ___ 10

0–5 points ☹	6–10 points 😐	11–15 points ☺
Too many mistakes – read this chapter again!	That was OK, but you can do better!	You did a really good job!

maximum number of points: ___ 15

5 Das Passiv

1 Check-up

Which sentences are *passive* and which are *active*? Circle the letters. All the letters together spell the name of a sport that was invented* in England.

*to invent – erfinden

Sentences	Active	Passive
Many different sports are played in Britain.	r	f
I have been playing polo for two hours.	o	u
In Britain pupils must do sports at school.	o	j
American Football is not played in Britain a lot.	p	t
Cricket has been played in many countries of the world since about the 19th century.	c	b
Sometimes rugby players are hurt.	l	a
Polo players wear special clothes.	l	t
Have you ever played polo?	l	k

f o o t b a l l was invented in England.

Das Passiv

Das Passiv wird immer dann verwendet, wenn man **nicht weiß, wer etwas gemacht** hat, oder wenn **es egal ist, wer etwas gemacht hat**. Das Passiv legt lediglich Wert darauf**, dass etwas überhaupt gemacht wurde oder passierte.**
Betrachte zum Beispiel folgenden Satz aus dem Check-up:

Aktiv	**Passiv**
Polo players **wear** special clothes.	Special clothes **are worn** in polo.
Hier sind die Spieler und ihr Aussehen wichtig.	Dies könnte zum Beispiel ein Sportartikelhersteller sagen, dem nur die Kleider wichtig sind.

Die Bildung des Passiv

Das Passiv wird gebildet mit dem Hilfsverb *sein (to be)* in der entsprechenden Zeitform und dem Verb im Partizip Perfekt:

Present tense	Rugby **is played** in Britain. Rugby **isn't played** in America. **Is** rugby **played** in Japan?
Present perfect	Cricket **has been played** here since the 19th century. Cricket **hasn't been played** here since the 19th century. **Has** cricket **been played** here since the 19th century?
Past tense	Football **was invented** in Britain. Football **wasn't invented** in China. **Was** football **invented** in France?
Will-future	Rugby **will be played** at school next Friday. Rugby **won't be played** at school next Friday. **Will** rugby **be played** at school next Friday?

Die Verwendung des Passiv

In manchen Situationen kann man entweder das Aktiv oder das Passiv verwenden, je nachdem, was man betonen möchte. Verwandelt man einen Satz vom Aktiv ins Passiv, verschwindet in der Regel das Subjekt des Aktiv-Satzes und das Objekt des Aktiv-Satzes wird zum Subjekt des Passiv-Satzes.

Subjekt	Verb	Objekt
The manager	fired	the coach.
The coach	was fired.	

Im Aktiv-Satz wird betont, wer den Trainer gefeuert hat, im Passiv-Satz ist lediglich wichtig, dass der Trainer weg ist – wer dafür verantwortlich ist, ist egal.

By-agent

Wenn man ausnahmsweise im Passiv doch einmal sagen möchte, wer etwas getan hat, verwendet man den sogenannten ***by-agent***. Dies kommt aber vergleichsweise selten vor. Nur wenn ein Passivsatz ohne *by-agent* sinnlos oder unverständlich ist, **muss** er verwendet werden. Bei der Umwandlung eines Aktiv-Satzes in einen Passiv-Satz wird dabei das Subjekt des Aktiv-Satzes zum ***by-agent***.

Subjekt	Verb	Objekt
The fans	ate	many sausages.
Many sausages	were eaten	by the fans.

5.1 *Irregular verbs*

Um das Passiv zu bilden, benötigst du das *past participle*. Dazu solltest du die unregelmäßigen Verben kennen. Hier kannst du einige von ihnen noch einmal wiederholen.

2

Complete the table, but be careful: there are a few regular verbs mixed in there.

Present tense	Simple past	Past participle
	drank	
burn		
		sold
spend		
play		
		thrown
	kept	
eat		
	wrote	
pay		
pull		
		broken
	saw	

5.2 Die Bildung des Passiv

3

Find all the passive forms in this text and underline them.

Sports in Britain

The British are crazy about sports, but many of their games are different from the ones that are played in Europe. Of course they like football. This game was invented in Britain in the last century. Today it is played everywhere. Then there is polo. In this game the ball is hit with sticks by people who sit on horses. Polo has always been played by the rich because they have enough money to buy horses. Rugby is loved in Britain, too. The ball looks like a big egg and is carried, thrown and kicked. The game is stopped for a moment when a player is thrown to the ground. Finally, there's cricket. Many people say that it is a lot like baseball, but it is much more difficult. A game can take a very long time. Sometimes it is even played for many days before there is a winner.

4

Correct these statements about British sports.

Example: Football was invented in France.
Football was invented in Britain.

1. Today football is played only in Northern England.

   ____

2. In polo the ball is hit with sticks by people who sit on cows.

   ____

3. In rugby the game is stopped for a moment when a player is killed.

   ____

4. A cricket game is very short. Sometimes it is only played for 15 minutes.

   ____

5

Now make negative sentences from these statements – they're all wrong.

Example: Football was invented in China.
Football wasn't invented in China.

1. In cricket, the ball is thrown from one player to the next.

   In cricket, the ball isn't thrown from one player to the next.

2. Polo has been played by the poor since it was invented.

   Polo hasn't been played by the poor since it was invented

3. Rugby is hated in Britain.

   Rugby isn't hated in Britain

4. Rugby is played with a big banana.

   ____

5. Cricket is usually played for a month before one team wins.

   ____

6

Ask questions about the text *Sports in Britain*. Make sure to use the correct tense.

Example: invent / where / football
Where was football invented?

1. invent / when / football?

____

2. football / play / where / today?

____

3. from where / hit / in polo / the ball?

____

4. the ball / kick / in rugby?

____

5. when / the game / stop / for a moment / in rugby?

____

6. cricket / for how long / sometimes / play?

____

7

The following text explains what happens at a football stadium. It is written in the *active* voice. Make a list of the things that **are done** at the stadium. Use the *passive* voice. You don't need a by-agent here.

At a football stadium

People who go to the stadium park their cars at a big car park or in the streets. At the entrance, assistants check the tickets, and guards search everybody for weapons or things that can be thrown. During the game a big screen shows all the exciting scenes again so everybody can see them. Fans of both teams sing a lot of songs to help their team. The shops sell a lot of beer and coke and the fans eat many sausages because singing makes so hungry and thirsty. After the game the assistants clean up the stadium and go home.

Example: *Cars are parked at a big car park or in the streets.*

1. At the entrance tickets are ______________________________.
2. At the entrance everybody ______________________________
   ______________________________.
3. All the exciting scenes ______________________________
   ______________________________.
4. A lot of songs ______________________________.
5. A lot of beer and coke ______________________________.
6. Many sausages ______________________________.
7. After the game ______________________________.

8

Put the sentences into the passive voice.

A group of crazy British rugby fans wants to make rugby the world's No. 1 sport. Here are their plans. After their meeting they make a list of all the things that **will be done**.

Example: "We will start our own homepage."
"Our own homepage will be started."

Plans for the future

1. "We will show all British rugby games on world wide television."
2. "We will organize important rugby games in every country of the world."
3. "We will start an international rugby fan club."
4. "Yes, and we will call it *Rugby Forever*."
5. "Good idea, and we will sell rugby balls all over the world."

9

Write down what **was done** in the stadium last year and what **has been done** recently.

Last year the Polo Club of Leicester had to close down. Nobody wanted to see a game in such an old stadium. Then a millionaire decided to make everything new.

Then and now

last year	now
simple past	**present perfect**
Example: lawn not mowed	new lawn put in
1. rubbish thrown onto the field	rubbish taken away and dustbins put up
2. sheep held in the stables[1]	horses put back into the stables
3. old cars left next to the field	old cars taken to the junk yard[2]
4. fish and chips kiosk destroyed	nice restaurant built

1 **stable** – Stall, 2 **junk yard** – Schrottplatz

Example:

Last year the lawn wasn't mowed but now a new lawn has been put in.

5.3 Der *by-agent*

10

Choose the correct *by-agent* for each gap.

A school in England is organizing a sports event. Here's the letter the headmistress wrote to the parents.

by helpful parents	**by the team captains**	**by myself**
by the best teams	**by some older pupils**	
by a teacher and a pupil	**by a supermarket**	

Dear parents,

Next week our great sports event of the year will take place. This year we want to give all the money we earn to charity. Rugby, football and cricket will be played. The teams will be led ______________________________ **(1)**. Of course food and drinks will be needed. We hope that cakes will be baked ______________________________ **(2)** and drinks will be donated* ______________________________ **(3)**. Of course the prizes will only be won ______________________________ **(4)** and will be bought ______________________________ **(5)**. Of course all the parents will want to watch the games, so little children and babies will be looked after ______________________________ **(6)**. In the end the money we have earned will be taken to a local charity organization ______________________________ **(7)** together. We hope that you will all come and have a great afternoon.

Yours sincerely,

Hedwig Galloway

(headmistress)

***to donate** – spenden

1

Correct the mistakes! There is one mistake in each sentence.

Example: Football is at first only played by men.
*Football **was** at first only played by men.*

1. Only in the late twentieth century have football been played by women, too.

   ____.

2. Today even world championships is organized for women.

   ____.

3. In America football will called "soccer".

   ____.

4. And there it isn't play by very many people.

   ____.

5. Are many games showed there on TV?

   ____?

6. Sport stars paid a lot of money.

   ____.

points: 6 *1 point for each correction*

2

Change the underlined sentences into the passive voice. Use a by-agent where necessary.

Active and passive teenagers

Everyday the newspapers write about children and teenagers who eat too much and don't do enough sports: "The school cafeterias sell them bad food! (1) Their parents put computers and televisions in their rooms! (2) They don't go for walks but sit at home all the time! At school the teachers don't teach their pupils about good food! (3) In short, nobody shows them what a healthy life is like (4)!" Now a young British cook has decided that this will change. "I will teach the cooks at the schools how to cook healthier," he says. "Then the teenagers will tell their parents about the good food at school. Then someone will instruct[1] the teachers (5), so they can teach their pupils about good food. This will be a great success," the young man says. Many people are excited, but others say it is not enough, and that the government has made too many mistakes in the past (6). It hasn't spent enough money on sports. (7) Nobody has repaired gymnasiums and sportsfields. (8) But the government is excited, too. "We will spend a lot of money now to help this young cook (9), and we will also hire[2] more sports teachers for the schools (10)," they say.

1 **to instruct** – to teach; 2 **to hire** – einstellen

2 points for each sentence; take one point off if you have used the wrong by-agent

points: 20

0–8 points ☹	9–16 points 😐	17–26 points ☺
Too many mistakes – read this chapter again!	That was OK, but you can do better!	You did a really good job!

maximum number of points: 26

Was ich bereits kann ...

Kreuze an, was für dich zutrifft.

	Kein Problem	Hier mache ich noch Fehler	Muss ich unbedingt noch üben
1 Bedingungssätze			
1. Ich kann *Conditional Sentences I* bilden.			
2. Ich kann *Conditional Sentences II* bilden.			
3. Ich weiß, wann man *Conditional Sentences I* und wann *Conditional Sentences II* verwendet.			
4. Ich kenne den Unterschied zwischen *if* und *when*.			
2 Gerundium und Infinitiv			
5. Ich weiß, was ein *gerund* ist und wann man es verwendet.			
6. Ich weiß, wann ich einen *infinitive* und wann ich ein *gerund* verwenden muss.			
3 Das *present perfect simple* und *progressive*			
7. Ich kann das *present perfect simple* bilden und weiß, wann man es verwendet.			
8. Ich kann das *present perfect progressive* bilden und weiß, wann man es verwendet.			
9. Ich kann entscheiden, ob ich das *present perfect simple* oder *progressive* verwenden muss.			

	Kein Problem	Hier mache ich noch Fehler	Muss ich unbedingt noch üben
4 Das *simple past* und das *past progressive*			
10. Ich kann das *simple past* bilden und weiß, wann man es verwendet.			
11. Ich kann das *past progressive* bilden und weiß, wann man es verwendet.			
12. Ich kann entscheiden, ob ich das *simple past* oder das *past progressive* verwenden muss.			
5 Das Passiv			
13. Ich kann das Passiv in allen wichtigen Zeiten bilden.			
14. Ich weiß, wann man das Passiv anwendet.			
15. Ich kann entscheiden, ob ich einen *by-agent* benötige oder nicht.			

Wortschatz

Hier wiederholst du

- notwendige Präpositionen und *phrasal verbs*
- wichtige Konjunktionen und
- tolle Methoden zum Vokabellernen

6 Präpositionen und *phrasal verbs*

6.1 Präpositionen

1 Check-up

Cross the odd one out.

on	after	under
in	into	next to
until	up	down
off	out of	on
under	until	during
after	before	around
into	from	out of
in front of	over	behind

Präpositionen

Präpositionen sind kleine Wörter, die man sehr oft falsch benutzt. Die meisten von ihnen sagen uns etwas über den Ort oder die Zeit, an dem oder während der die Handlung unseres Satzes stattfindet. Oft wird die Bedeutung der Präposition erst klar, wenn man sie im Zusammenhang mit anderen Wörtern im Satz sieht:

Let's meet **on Sunday**.
Let's meet **on the bridge**.

Im ersten Satz bedeutet *on* „am". Es gehört zu *Sunday* und gibt die Zeit an. Im zweiten bedeutet es „auf". Es gehört zu *the bridge* und gibt den Ort an. Die Präposition *on* kann also sowohl in Orts- als auch in Zeitangaben verwendet werden.
Dies ist bei anderen Präpositionen wie z. B. *during*, *under*, *after* nicht der Fall. Sie können nur entweder mit Orts- (*under*) oder mit Zeitangaben (*during, after*) verwendet werden.

2

Read the description of Hannah's room and draw the items, or write their names in the right places.

Hannah's room

Hannah's room is not very tidy. Her chair is on her bed and the dustbin lies next to the desk. On her desk she has got a dirty sock and her lamp is under the desk. Between her desk and her bed is a stereo, but all around the stereo are her CDs. She likes animals a lot. That's why she has put up a poster of a horse on the wall over her bed – but it's upside down. The poster of her favourite hip hop-band was on the door so she could say "goodbye" to them when she left, but now it's on the floor in front of the door. On her bookshelf she has got her trainers and under the trainers she put her schoolbooks. Next to the schoolbooks and the trainers she has got a box. This box is very important. She puts all her treasures[1] into it: her earrings, her necklace[2], and her letters. That's why it's really the only thing that's in its right place.

1 **treasure** – Schatz; 2 **necklace** – Halskette

3

The prepositions of time got mixed up in this text. Cross them out and complete the sentences with the correct prepositions.

Hannah's first day of the school year

During ______________ **(1)** Monday she goes to school and meets all her friends. **After** ______________ **(2)** the school day she finds out about her new schedule and the new teachers. **Until** ______________ **(3)** school she goes to the shops and buys all the new exercise books, and **in** ______________ **(4)** that she meets her friends at the best ice-cream place in town. When she gets home late **on** ______________ **(5)** the afternoon, she sits in front of the telephone and waits **after** ______________ **(6)** it is five o'clock. That's when her best friend Marie always calls. **At** ______________ **(7)** the evening she has dinner with her parents and **in** ______________ **(8)** night she dreams about another great day without homework.

4

Complete the sentences using the prepositions from the list below.

into **around** **at** **at** **down** **to** **out** **at** **at** **outside** **to** **at** **from** **on** **into** **in front of** **at** **to** **at** **to** **for** **out of** **until**

A normal day at school for Hannah

In the mornings Hannah steps ________________ (1) the door ________________ (2) 8:30. School starts ________________ (3) 9:30 a.m. She walks ________________ (4) the street ________________ (5) about five minutes until she gets ________________ (6) the bus stop. There she meets some of her friends. Together they climb ________________ (7) the bus and sit down ________________ (8) the back. Then they take ________________ (9) their homework and compare what they have done. Sometimes one of the girls doesn't have her homework. Then she copies it ________________ (10) her friends. When they arrive ________________ (11) school, they quickly go ________________ (12) their classroom to meet their other friends. When their teacher walks ________________ (13) the room they all put their exercise books ________________ (14) the desks and say "Good morning." Their teachers usually stand ________________ (15) the blackboard but sometimes they also walk ________________ (16) the classroom to look ________________ (17) the pupils' exercises or to talk ________________ (18) them. ________________ (19) the end of the lesson the teachers usually give them homework – Hannah hates that, because when she comes home, she has to go ________________ (20) her room and sit down ________________ (21) her desk to do her homework ________________ (22) six o'clock. Then her parents let her go ________________ (23) and meet her friends.

6.2 *Phrasal verbs*

5 Check-up

Match the sentences to the correct picture.

1.

2.

3.

4.

5.

6.

Sentence	No.
The teacher is putting his books into the bag.	
She is filling in a worksheet.	
"Please look after our goldfish while we are away with our tutor group!"	
He is putting on his trainers for PE.	
They're looking at a map.	
They are getting on the bus.	

Verben mit Präpositionen – *phrasal verbs*

Manche Verben sind mit einer bestimmten Präposition oder einem Adverb sozusagen verwachsen. Die Präposition gehört zu diesem Verb dazu und steht (fast immer) direkt dahinter. Lässt man sie weg oder verändert man sie, verändert sich auch die Bedeutung des Satzes oder aber er verliert seinen Sinn.

Einige dieser Verben hast du in Übung 4 wahrscheinlich schon automatisch richtig ergänzt. Andere ***phrasal verbs*** sind jedoch schwieriger. Folgende ***phrasal verbs*** kannst du in diesem Kapitel üben:

to look **for**	suchen
to look **at**	anschauen
to look **after**	sich kümmern um
to look something **up**	etwas nachschauen
to put something **in(to)**	etwas in etwas hineinlegen
to put something **on**	etwas anziehen; etwas auf etwas darauflegen
to put something **up**	etwas aufhängen
to take something **off**	etwas ausziehen, abhängen, z. B. von der Wand
to fill something **in**	etwas ausfüllen
to get **on**	einsteigen; auf etwas hinaufsteigen
to get **off**	aussteigen, heruntersteigen, verlassen
to get **up**	aufstehen
to get **in(to)**	in etwas hineingehen
to turn something **on**	einschalten
to turn something **off**	ausschalten
to turn something **up**	lauter stellen

Wie du siehst, gibt es ***phrasal verbs***, die nur aus Verb und Präposition bestehen, und solche, die zusätzlich noch ein Objekt (something, somebody) haben. Bei diesen kann man sich die Satzstellung in der Regel aussuchen:

He picked the bag **up**.
He picked **up** the bag.

Beides ist richtig. Da es aber Sonderfälle gibt, empfehlen wir dir immer die erste Möglichkeit zu wählen, da sie fast immer richtig ist. (Nur wenn das Objekt so lang ist, dass man den Satz sonst nicht mehr versteht, muss das Objekt hinter die Präposition).

6

Complete the table. Use the phrasal verbs and your own information (time, place, etc.).

What you do in the morning

Phrasal verb	**It's time to get up**
get up	*I get up at 7 o'clock.*
turn on (radio)	
take off (pyjamas)	
get in (shower)	
turn on / off (water)	
put on (clothes)	
look at (myself / mirror)	
put into (books)	
Then I have breakfast in the kitchen.	
get on (bike / bus)	
get off	
look for (friends, playground)	

7

Write down what the people in the picture are doing. Use the phrasal verbs and the objects given.

At the drama club: it is two hours before the first performance*. All the pupils are very busy.

*__performance__ – Aufführung

At the drama club

~~look for / his coat (Michael)~~ – look at / himself in the mirror (John)
look up / her text in the textbook (Andrea) – turn on / the lights (Alice)
put into / a pistol / a box (Hannah) – get off / the stage (Mrs. Miller)
take off / her wig* (Khavita) – turn up / the music (Jill)
put on / his costume (Philip)

*wig – Perücke

Example: *Michael is looking for his coat.*

1. ______________________________

2. ______________________________

3. ______________________________

4. ______________________________

5. ______________________________

6. ______________________________

7. ______________________________

8. ______________________________

8 9

Complete the sentences below using the correct phrasal verb from the box. You can listen to the CD to check your answers.

At the computer club: Shawn is new at the club and the other pupils are helping him.

put in	look after	look for
look at (2x)	turn off	
put up (2x)	fill in	look up

At the computer club

Shawn: I'm ____________ (1) a website about Germany. Can someone help me please?

Synn: Oh that's easy, Shawn, just go to "Google" and ____________ (2) "Germany".

Shawn: Wow, ____________ (3) this! It's all in German. There are so many words I don't understand.

Andrea: You can ____________ them ____________ (4) in an online dictionary or you can translate the pages with this button.

Shawn: Oops, that translation is crazy. It's so funny. We should ____________ it ____________ (5) on the wall, so other pupils can ____________ (6) it.

Andrea: Look, I've found a page that asks English teenagers for their opinions about Germany. Will anyone help me to ________ it ______ **(7)**?

Synn: Yes, that will be fun – and when we're done, we can print it out and ________ it ______ **(8)** on the wall next to the crazy translation.

Shawn: Oh, time's up already. That was lots of fun. Now I must __________ my computer __________ **(9)**. But I love it now. It's great. I can't wait until tomorrow. Who will ________________________ **(10)** it while I'm at home?

Tom: Don't worry about it Shawn. Computers are great, but they don't need a babysitter.

1

Cross out the wrong preposition.

1. Hannah usually gets up **on / at** 7:30.
2. She meets her friends **on / at** the bus station.
3. She hates homework because she has to do it **until / after** school.
4. Hannah's friends usually meet **in / at** the evenings.
5. They like to meet **before / in front of** an ice cream place.
6. Then they go **inside / outside** and eat a lot.
7. They leave **after / behind** they have paid and go home.

points: 3,5 *0,5 point for each preposition*

2

Complete the list. Which prepositions tell you about time, and which about places? Be careful, because some of them fit in both lists.

on – under – in – into – out of – after – down – up – to – around – at – over – during – until – before

Place	Time

points: 9,5 *0,5 point for each correct entry*

3

Hannah writes to her German pen friend about the German lesson she had yesterday.
Every sentence contains a phrasal verb.

3.1

First find and underline the phrasal verbs.

1 point for each phrasal verb *points:* 9

3.2

Only four of them are correct. Find the five other ones and correct the mistakes.

1 point for each correction *points:* 5

Hi Anita,
We had a very strange German lesson yesterday. At the beginning of the lesson Mr. Jenkins opened his bag and started to look after something. About one minute later he found it – a real bunny. The bunny got onto the desk and just sat there. We were all sitting at our desks and looked the bunny up. While we were waiting, Mr. Jenkins put a colourful coat on and started to talk to the bunny in German. That was strange, but then the bunny answered. A bunny that speaks German – wow. Then Mr. Jenkins turned the cassette recorder off and the bunny got off the desk and started to dance. It was a German song and the bunny danced until Mr. Jenkins turned the music on again. After the lesson Mr. Jenkins told us that his parents owned a circus and that they had taught him a lot of tricks. Our homework is terrible, though: we have to take our German dictionaries and have to look at all the words about pets. That's what I must do now.

Bye bye
Hannah

0–13 points ☹	14–21 points 😐	22–27 points ☺
Too many mistakes – read this chapter again!	That was OK, but you can do better!	You did a really good job!

maximum number of points: 27

7 Konjunktionen

1 Check-up

In each sentence of the short text below there is at least one conjunction. Underline them.

Sarah's birthday

Sarah was looking forward to Tuesday next week because it was her 13th birthday. Her mother made her a birthday cake and woke her up at six o'clock a.m., because they always do that in her family when it is somebody's birthday. Sarah was very excited although it was so early in the morning. As soon as she got downstairs, she ran into the kitchen to look at all the presents she got and spent time opening them until she had to go to school. Of course she forgot to eat breakfast.

Konjunktionen machen Sprache spannend

Stell dir diesen Text einmal ohne die **Konjunktionen** vor:

"Sarah was looking forward to Tuesday next week. It was her 13th birthday. Her mother made her a birthday cake. She woke Sarah up at six o'clock a.m. They always do that in her family …"

Ziemlich langweilig und eintönig, oder? **Konjunktionen** dienen dazu, Sätze miteinander zu verbinden und sinnvolle Zusammenhänge herzustellen – warum freute sich Sarah? Warum hat ihre Mutter einen Kuchen gebacken? Sie haben deshalb einen großen Einfluss auf die Bedeutung des Satzes. Vergleiche dazu diese beiden folgenden Sätze:

1. Sarah was very excited **although** it was so early in the morning.
2. Sarah was very excited **because** it was so early in the morning.

Im ersten Satz scheint Sarah den frühen Morgen generell eher nicht zu schätzen, im zweiten ist das Gegenteil der Fall.
In diesem Kapitel kannst du üben, Konjunktionen im Englischen richtig zu verwenden.
Die folgende Übersicht zeigt dir, welche wichtigen Konjunktionen in diesem Kapitel geübt werden.

Wichtige Konjunktionen und ihre Bedeutung

Konjunktion	Funktion (Welchen Zusammenhang stellt sie her?)	Stellung im Satz
although (obwohl)	gibt Gegensätze an	Können auch am Satzanfang verwendet werden. Verbinden Haupt- und Nebensatz.
when (als, wenn)	gibt an, dass etwas gleichzeitig passiert	
as soon as (sobald)	gibt an, dass etwas sofort auf etwas anderes folgt	
until (bis)	gibt an, dass etwas aufhört bis etwas anderes passiert	

Konjunktion	Funktion (Welchen Zusammenhang stellt sie her?)	Stellung im Satz
after **(nachdem)**	gibt an, dass etwas passiert, nachdem etwas anderes passiert ist	Kann auch am Satzanfang verwendet werden. Verbindet Haupt- und Nebensatz.
because **(weil)**	gibt Gründe an	Werden nie am Satzanfang verwendet. Verbinden Haupt- und Nebensatz.
so that **(so dass)**	stellt eine Konsequenz (Folge) dar	
and **(und)**	stellt zwei gleichwertige Haupt- oder Nebensätze nebeneinander	Wird nie am Satzanfang verwendet. Verbindet zwei Haupt- oder zwei Nebensätze.
but **(aber)**	stellt Widersprüche dar	Wird nie am Satzanfang verwendet. Kann entweder Haupt- und Nebensatz oder aber zwei Haupt- oder Nebensätze verbinden.

Ein Komma setzt man im Englischen normalerweise nur, wenn der Nebensatz mit der Konjunktion am Anfang steht:

Sarah was very excited **although** it was early in the morning.
Although it was early in the morning**,** Sarah was very excited.

7.1 Die richtige Konjunktion auswählen

2

Mark the correct conjunction. Sometimes both are possible.

What to give to Sarah

1. *Philip:* I would like to get her the new CD by her favourite pop-group **and / but** she has got it already.
2. *Sandra:* You know, I have bought her a lipstick **although / but** she's got about ten of them already.
3. *Andrea:* That's not the same thing, Sandra, **because / so that** you can always use a lipstick. I will not buy a present **as soon as / until** I know what everybody else has bought.
4. *George:* That's very clever, Andrea. I will buy one **as soon as / when** I see the right one in some shop.
5. *Fiona:* I don't think that's a good idea **because / although** you never go to the shops, George.
6. *Ben:* I will get her a German dictionary **as soon as / so that** her German will get better.
7. *Brenda:* I think her German won't get better **and / until** she sits down and does her homework. That's why I will get her an organizer.
8. *Andrew:* I will just give her a kiss **although / because** I'm sure she will love that present a lot.
9. *Sandra:* Oh yes, and I think **after / because** you have kissed her she will fall asleep and never wake up again.
10. *Andrew:* Right. She will sleep for one hundred years **after / until** a beautiful prince comes along to kiss her again. This will be a great birthday!

3

Cross out the conjunctions that don't work. In some cases, two of the three conjunctions will be correct, but the meaning of the sentence might change.

What Sarah would like

1. Hm, I would really like a new bike **although / because / so that** I can get to school faster and sleep longer.
2. Sleeping longer in the mornings will be great **although / but / because** I have to be careful not to sleep too long.
3. I would love to have another lipstick **until / so that / although** I have eleven in my bathroom.
4. Lipsticks are very useful **until / after / when** I go to parties.
5. I think I will wait forever for a new computer **because / and / but** that's OK because they are very expensive.
6. My parents are very good at choosing presents **because / when / until** they have enough time to look for them.
7. I just hope that Andrew won't kiss me **because / after / when** he comes to my party.
8. If he does that, everybody will look at me **but / and / as soon as** I will go crazy.
9. I will spend a hundred hours with my new presents **until / as soon as / when** all my friends have left my party.

7.2 Sätze mit Konjunktionen bilden

4

Make sentences using the sentence machine below. Sometimes more than one solution is possible.

Trouble with birthday presents

- I hate birthdays
- Philip loves birthdays
- I never buy presents
- The Millers buy nice presents
- Alice is always in a good mood
- Jill and Brenda are very sad
- I will sing her a love song
- Andrew wants to go to the party
- Sarah will say “thank you” to her parents

- because
- until
- although
- when
- but
- as soon as
- so that
- and
- after

- the party is over.
- it's almost too late.
- she is invited to a birthday party.
- he wants to kiss Sarah.
- they don't spend much money on them.
- they aren't invited to the birthday party.
- she will kiss me.
- he is good at choosing presents.
- I never know what to buy.

1. ______________________________

   ____

2. ______________________________

   ____

3. ______________________________

   ____

4. ______________________________

   ____

5. ______________________________

   ____

6. ______________________________

____

7. ______________________________

____

8. ______________________________

____

9. ______________________________

____

5

Rewrite the following sentences with the subordinate clause at the beginning.

Birthday presents – yes or no?

Example:
Birthday presents are important although they are sometimes expensive.
Although birthday presents are sometimes expensive, they are important.

1. We shouldn't give presents until we are sure we really like the person.

____

____

2. I usually buy a present as soon as I'm invited to a party.

____

____

3. I never bought birthday presents when I was thirteen.

____

____

4. I will never buy birthday presents for my parents although they usually give me a lot of presents for my birthday.

____

____

6

In this text all the conjunctions are wrong. Cross out the wrong conjunctions and rewrite the text so that it makes sense. Be careful – sometimes more than one conjunction is possible.

Sarah's mother goes out to buy a present

One week before Sarah's birthday her mother went to the city centre although she wanted to find a few birthday presents for her daughter. Because she parked her car, she had a good idea: "Maybe we can buy her a bike until she can get to school faster. That's good but then she will have more time for breakfast." But Sarah's mother went into the shopping mall, she saw a shop for motorcycles and thought: "We won't buy her a motorcycle when she is 18." Then she saw a shop for make-up. She went inside and thought: "She loves lipsticks but wants to look nice at parties." Then she went on and found a bicycle-shop. So that she saw a shop assistant, she asked him for a bike for her daughter after he showed her one that she liked. But it was very expensive, she bought it as soon as went home – she was very excited.

7

All of the conjunctions have been left out of this text. Use conjunctions to complete and connect the sentences. (* = there's a conjunction missing here.)

Sarah's father went shopping, too

1. Sarah's father went shopping that day, too. * He went to a different part of town.

   Sarah's father went shopping that day, too, but / although he went to a different part of town.

2. He works a lot. * He and his wife didn't have much time to plan the birthday shopping.

   ____

   ____

3. He thought: "We have to buy Sarah a new bike. * Her bike is much too small for her now.

4. She will like that. * Then she will be able to sleep longer in the mornings."

5. * he saw a make-up shop, he thought:

6. "I will not buy a new lipstick for her. * She already has got about thirty in her bathroom."

7. Then Sarah's father was very hungry. * He went to the food court and ordered a pizza.

8. * he left the shopping centre a few minutes later, he had a good idea.

9. I will buy a new German computer programme for her. * She can get better marks at school.

1 10

Complete the sentences using the correct conjunction(s). Often more than one is possible.

After her birthday, Sarah talks to her friends about her birthday presents.

Sarah: My parents are crazy ________________ **(1)** they bought two bikes for me.

Andrea: That's strange ________________ **(2)** it's also good. Now you can sell one bike and buy something else for the money.

George: Yes, ________________ **(3)** you've sold the bike, you should buy a computer with the money.

Sarah: I will have to wait a long time ________________ **(4)** I find a computer that's cheap enough. Maybe I will save the money ________________ **(5)** I can buy something nice in a year or so. I also got two lipsticks. That's good ________________ **(6)** I only have ten and it's always good to have different colours.

George: Do you like the German computer programme?

Sarah: Yes, I like it a lot ________________ **(7)** it doesn't work on my computer, haha.

Andrea: You know, ________________ **(8)** it doesn't work, I think it's a nice present. Your father wants to help you ________________ **(9)** you get better marks, and that's nice, isn't it?

George: Sarah, did Andrew really kiss you? He said he wanted to ________________ **(10)** we were talking about birthday presents.

Sarah: Yes, he did. He came to me ________________ **(11)** everybody started dancing. Ughhhhh.

1 point for each correct conjunction *points:* 16

2

If possible, rewrite the following sentences with the subordinate clause at the beginning.

Sarah is thinking about her next birthday.

1. I will invite Andrew although he kissed me this year.

____

____

2. I will not let my parents go shopping next year until they have talked to each other about my presents.

____

____

3. I will invite more people so that I will get more presents than this year.

____

____

4. I will give a little present to every guest when they arrive.

____

____

5. My next birthday will be great but I hope I won't get another bicycle.

____

____

points: 5 *1 point for each sentence*

3

Choose two clauses and connect them with a conjunction. Write at least 9 sentences. You must use some clauses more than once.

- Birthdays are great
- Parties are great for the parents, too
- Sarah helped her parents clean up the house
- Sarah didn't use her new German programme
- The next day Sarah used her new lipstick
- Buying presents is fun
- The next day at school Andrew didn't kiss her
- Sarah was very happy

- you get a lot of presents.
- she got another bad mark in a German test.
- they cost a lot of money.
- they must do all the work.
- rode her bike to school.
- he smiled at her.
- her friends left.
- when Andrew kissed her again a week later.

1 point for each sentence *points:* 9

0–15 points ☹	16–24 points 😐	25–30 points ☺
Too many mistakes – read this chapter again!	That was OK, but you can do better!	You did a really good job!

maximum number of points: 30

8 Tipps zum Lernen von Vokabeln

1 Check-up

Look for ten things you can find in a house. Look for them up and down and across!

S	f	y	z	u	d	l	c	f	a	d	b	m
e	t	e	l	e	v	i	s	i	o	n	j	i
y	d	e	z	u	h	g	p	l	e	p	o	r
e	f	t	w	s	t	j	x	w	l	p	e	r
l	i	v	i	n	g	r	o	o	m	i	d	o
a	f	e	z	l	a	m	p	r	r	l	g	r
a	c	v	n	d	s	e	s	d	r	l	z	t
s	u	h	i	q	j	m	d	j	g	o	f	a
e	p	u	k	i	t	c	h	e	n	w	o	i
c	b	u	s	i	l	o	a	w	r	u	k	s
o	o	u	y	t	t	w	z	j	i	d	h	t
e	a	e	s	d	j	c	u	p	d	k	r	a
a	r	j	o	l	p	c	u	j	i	p	r	i
p	d	g	f	d	w	i	o	e	d	j	u	r
c	h	u	a	e	a	j	u	o	n	e	h	s

Vokabeln lernen – die reine Qual?

Vokabellernen ist eine der schwierigsten und mühsamsten Aufgaben beim Erlernen einer Fremdsprache. Es gibt aber Möglichkeiten, dies **erfolgreicher und abwechslungsreicher** zu gestalten, als immer nur deutsch – englisch – englisch – deutsch auswendig zu lernen.

Generell gilt: **Gib jedem Wort einen Zusammenhang** und du wirst es dir besser merken können. Das folgende Kapitel zeigt dir einige Wege, wie du Wörter in einen Zusammenhang stellen kannst, und übt dies an drei wichtigen Wortfeldern *(At home, On the phone, At the shops)*. Viele der Wörter, mit denen geübt wird, kennst du vermutlich bereits, andere sind möglicherweise neu. Wahrscheinlich wirst du die unbekannten mit Hilfe der Übungen verstehen. Wenn nicht, schlage sie einfach in deinem Wörterbuch nach.

Techniken zum Erlernen von Vokabeln

1. **Das Wort wird mit einem Bild oder einem Ort in Verbindung gebracht**. Du kannst dir zu Hause auch Zettel mit Vokabeln an bestimmte Orte hängen und dir Wörter dadurch besser merken.
2. **Das Wort wird im Satzzusammenhang verwendet** (so lernt man auch gleich, wie man es verwendet). Dabei hilft dir in der Regel auch dein Schulbuch. Die mittlere Spalte im Vokabelteil gibt dir in der Regel einen Satz, in dem die Vokabel vorkommt. Ist dies nicht der Fall, kannst du einfach selbst einen schreiben.
3. **Das Wort wird zusammen mit Wörtern gelernt, mit denen es häufig vorkommt.** (z. B. *to answer the phone*)
4. **Wörter werden in Gruppen, Familien oder Wortarten (z. B Adjektiv, Nomen, Verb) eingeteilt**.
5. **Man merkt sich gleich bestimmte kurze Sätze**, die so – oder so ähnlich – häufig vorkommen.
6. **Wörter anwenden und umsetzen!**
   Besonders wichtig ist, dass du das gelernte Vokabular möglichst oft anwendest. Dazu gibt es viele Möglichkeiten, z. B.:
   - Gute mündliche Mitarbeit im Unterricht
   - Lesen englischer Bücher, Zeitschriften, Internetseiten etc.
   - Brief- oder Mailkontakt zu Jugendlichen in englischsprachigen Ländern
   - Englisches Fernsehen und Radio

8.1 Zu Hause

2

Put the letters in the correct order and write down what the objects in the picture are called.

Helen's house

Küche:

1. kins
2. roferirgater
3. slags
4. upc
5. talep
6. cowaivmer
7. rezeref

Bad:

9. hewors
9. oliett
10. wolet
11. potothesta
12. botothursh
13. poas

Wohnzimmer:

14. chouc
15. oreest
16. enoph
17. criarham
18. efefoc latbe

Schlafzimmer:

19. edb
20. lowlip
21. ajamyps

3

Complete the sentences using the correct verb from the box.

What Helen does in her house

set	**go**	**do**	**answer**	**take**
switch on	**relax**	**have**	**brush**	**switch off**

1. She ________________ the dishes in the sink.
2. She ________________ the stereo ______ when she wants to listen to music.
3. She ________________ the coffee table when her friends come to visit her.
4. She ________________ the phone when it rings.
5. She ________________ on the couch after school.
6. She ________________ breakfast every morning.
7. She ________________ a shower every morning before she goes to school.
8. She ________________ her teeth three times a day with her toothbrush.
9. She ________________ all the lights ______ in the house before she ________________ to bed.

4

Complete the table using the words below.

In the kitchen

plate
cheese
spoon
butter
glass
microwave oven
sausage
dishwasher
juice
stove
fork
refrigerator
milk
knife
coffeemaker
freezer
lemonade
blender

In the cupboard	In the refrigerator	Machines that help you

5

Choose the correct answer(s) – sometimes more than one is correct.

1. You use a stereo to
   - ☐ a) watch TV.
   - ☐ b) listen to music.
   - ☐ c) write emails.

2. You … a toilet.
   - ☐ a) do
   - ☐ b) take
   - ☐ c) use

3. You … a bath.
   - ☐ a) take
   - ☐ b) have
   - ☐ c) sit

4. You use a sink to
   - ☐ a) keep your food cool.
   - ☐ b) take a shower.
   - ☐ c) wash your hands.

5. The alarm clock goes off when
   - ☐ a) you have to get up in the morning.
   - ☐ b) somebody breaks into the house.
   - ☐ c) a fire breaks out in the house.

6. You usually drink water from a
   - ☐ a) glass.
   - ☐ b) cup.
   - ☐ c) bottle.

7. In the evening you go … bed.
   - ☐ a) in
   - ☐ b) into
   - ☐ c) to

8. In the morning you … breakfast.
   - ☐ a) hurry
   - ☐ b) have
   - ☐ c) eat

8.2 Am Telefon

6

Complete the conversation by giving the sentences numbers and putting them in the correct order. After you have done the exercise, listen to the CD to check your answers.

1. Helen and her friend 11

- [ ] "Sure. Hang on a minute."
- [ ] "Bye Susan."
- [ ] "OK, then I'll go by myself. Bye Helen."
- [ ] "Hi, Susan. What's up?"
- [ ] "No, I'm too tired. I was up late last night. There was a great party at Edward's house."
- [ ] "Hi Dan, this is Susan. Can I speak to Helen, please?"
- [1] "Hello, Luton 3461394, Dan Mitchel speaking."
- [ ] "Not much. I just wanted to ask you if we're going running this afternoon."

2. Helen and the doctor's office 12

- [ ] "Yes, could you please ask her to call me back."
- [ ] "Good afternoon. This is Helen Mitchel speaking. May I speak to Dr. Miller, please?"
- [ ] "Good bye."
- [ ] "Dr. Miller's practice, Nurse Dana speaking. How may I help you?"
- [ ] "Hold on a minute … I'm sorry, but Dr. Miller is very busy at the moment. May I take a message?"
- [ ] "Thank you very much. Good bye."
- [ ] "Certainly, Mrs. Mitchel. Dr. Miller will ring you as soon as possible."

7

In the first dialogue Helen is talking to a friend. In the second she is talking to a person she doesn't know.

Complete the table below by sorting the two different types of words into the correct column.

Informal (to a friend)	Formal (to a stranger)
hi	*good afternoon*
	How may I help you?

8

Complete the sentences using the correct words from the box. After you have done the exercise, listen to the CD to check your answers.

Answering machines

1. What answering machines tell you 13

from	as soon as	call	answer	number	
to	message	visit	reached	home	closed

1. Hi, this is Andrew's machine. Leave a __________ after the beep.

2. Hello, you've reached the Millers. Sorry, we're not __________ right now, but if you leave a message, we will __________ you back as soon as possible.

3. Hello. This is Mrs. Anderson's office. We can't __________ the phone right now, but please leave your name and __________ and we will call you back __________ possible.

4. Hello. You've __________ "Shoes and More" in Bond Street. We are __________ in the mornings. Our opening hours are __________ 1 p.m. __________ 8 p.m. daily. We look forward to your __________.

2. What you say to answering machines 14

worry	question	like	call	could	this
minutes	ill	number	let's	at	thank

1. Hi, Alice, __________ is Helen. Something really exciting happened at school today. __________ me back soon!

2. Good afternoon, this is Mr. Briand. I have got a __________ about my son's class test. __________ you please call me back. My __________ is 020-01324984. Thank you very much.

3. Hey Andy, __________ go to the park today to play some football. I'll be there in 20 __________. Don't __________ about the English homework, Mr. Miller is __________.

4. Good morning. I would __________ to order two tickets for "Dracula's Return" tonight __________ 6 p.m. My number is 020-20457653. __________ you, good bye.

Now listen to the people returning the calls from exercise 8.2 "What you say to answering machines" and mark the correct answers.

3. What people say when they call back

1. Alice 15

- ☐ a) is very excited because she got good marks on a history test.
- ☐ b) had been out biking when Helen called.
- ☐ c) has been asked out by a boy from form 10.
- ☐ d) wants to go to a football match with Helen and the boys on Saturday.
- ☐ e) hopes that Helen has been asked out by Matt.

2. The teacher 16

- ☐ a) thinks that Mr. Briand's son is very good at school.
- ☐ b) wants Mr. Briand to call back as soon as possible.
- ☐ c) believes that there is no need to talk because there is no hope left for Mr. Briand's son.
- ☐ d) wants to organize some extra help for Mr. Briand's son.
- ☐ e) invites Mr. Briand to his office on Tuesday.

3. Andy 17

- ☐ a) is very surprised that Mr. Miller is ill.
- ☐ b) is very unhappy that Mr. Miller is ill.
- ☐ c) will do his homework anyway because he thinks English is important.
- ☐ d) wants to go to the shops later.
- ☐ e) thinks that his mother likes ego-shooters.

4. The tickets for "Dracula's Return" 18

- ☐ a) have all been sold.
- ☐ b) are 6 pounds apiece.
- ☐ c) can be bought for tomorrow's performance at 9 p.m.
- ☐ d) can be bought for tomorrow's performance at 8 p.m.
- ☐ e) can only be bought on the black market for 15 pounds or more.

8.3 Im Geschäft

9

There are 24 verbs, adjectives and nouns hidden in the grid – find them and write them in the list.
All the words have something to do with shopping. Be careful, some of them are made up of two words!

s	h	o	p	s	l	e	r	g	a	h	g	u	j	s	o	r	l
u	d	z	s	h	o	n	i	t	r	y	o	n	c	t	u	l	l
p	a	h	z	o	o	e	j	i	p	s	w	l	o	t	a	e	r
e	c	g	t	p	k	i	z	r	o	w	t	e	w	m	e	i	t
r	o	z	r	a	f	e	d	n	b	o	o	k	s	t	o	r	e
m	y	r	e	s	o	j	u	c	i	e	h	u	o	r	x	g	j
a	o	l	e	s	r	q	t	o	f	c	z	b	j	e	v	j	o
r	s	h	i	i	k	l	o	s	b	f	e	s	a	g	u	i	o
k	o	u	t	s	v	h	u	t	l	a	r	z	t	k	r	e	w
e	j	g	c	t	e	u	i	o	u	y	c	f	r	z	e	i	r
t	m	h	z	a	m	t	r	t	w	z	t	r	e	w	h	r	j
g	g	h	j	n	u	i	i	o	z	r	e	w	r	z	u	o	y
d	i	k	t	t	p	f	s	f	f	h	j	k	l	d	j	i	o
e	a	f	t	z	u	d	g	l	o	o	k	a	r	o	u	n	d
p	i	m	t	l	r	w	s	f	h	z	e	s	x	g	j	i	s
a	x	g	h	s	u	i	o	c	u	t	r	e	i	l	d	r	e
r	c	h	t	z	h	i	o	h	o	h	u	r	x	d	f	u	l
t	t	i	z	r	l	o	t	u	t	o	l	p	s	r	e	w	l
m	v	g	h	z	h	l	p	t	h	e	l	p	x	d	h	z	u
e	n	k	i	s	h	o	e	s	t	o	r	e	m	u	t	e	d
n	r	t	k	s	g	l	o	h	j	b	u	y	n	r	z	e	a
t	g	e	i	t	e	i	m	n	v	s	g	t	r	j	r	r	z
s	a	s	k	k	z	r	s	u	o	z	l	l	v	r	l	s	t
t	l	i	z	r	n	i	c	e	f	v	y	c	h	e	a	p	d
o	v	h	z	u	i	s	w	c	b	h	n	u	i	a	r	c	f
r	j	t	e	s	e	t	u	l	s	e	v	n	n	t	g	r	t
e	x	p	e	n	s	i	v	e	s	f	t	w	k	u	e	k	o

Nouns
book store

Adjectives
beautiful

Verbs
try on

10

Fill in the gaps. Use words from exercise 9.

At the ____________________

Shop assistant:	Good morning, may I help you?
You:	Yes please. I'm ______________________ some new shoes.
Shop assistant:	Alright, let's see. Yes, I've got some very _________________ ones over here. How do you like them?
You:	Not so much. How about those over there, they look really ____________________.
Shop assistant:	Would you like to ______________ them _______? What's your size?
You:	My shoe size is 5½, but could you first tell me how much they ______________, please?
Shop assistant:	They are 80 pounds.
You:	Wow, that's too ____________________ for me. Have you got some cheaper ones, too?
Shop assistant:	I'm sorry, these are the cheapest shoes we have.
You:	Well, I think I will have to look somewhere else then. Good bye.
Shop assistant:	Good bye.

11

What can you buy at which store? Complete the table.

Supermarket	Bakery

Book store	Gift shop

bread
CD
pen
milk
postcard
butter
teddy bear
map
fish
crisps
chocolate
lipstick
magazine
book
vegetables
fruit
poster
cake

12

Find the correct English expression for each situation.

What to say at the shops

Situation	Nr.
Du lehnst die Hilfe eines Verkäufers ab und sagst ihm, dass du dich nur ein wenig umschauen möchtest.	
Du verabschiedest dich freundlich aus dem Geschäft.	
Du fragst die Verkäuferin, ob sie dasselbe Produkt noch eine Nummer kleiner hat.	
Du bringst deine Begeisterung über eine Farbe zum Ausdruck.	
Du bittest höflich um Hilfe.	
Du fragst höflich, ob du ein bestimmtes T-Shirt anprobieren darfst.	
Du bedankst dich und sagst, dass du es dir noch einmal überlegen möchtest.	
Du fragst den Verkäufer, ob er nicht etwas Ähnliches billiger anzubieten hat.	
Du fragst, wo du die Milch finden kannst.	
Du bittest die Verkäuferin, dir beim Suchen nach einem Geschenk für einen Freund zu helfen.	

1

There is one mistake in each sentence. Find it and correct it.

1. In the morning Helen's computer goes off and she gets up and takes a shower.

 ____

2. Helen uses toothpaste to wash her hands.

 ____

3. Before breakfast she takes the plates from the refrigerator and puts them on the table.

 ____

4. After that she puts lemonade into the coffee maker and sits down.

 ____

5. When Helen leaves the house, she switches all the lights on.

 ____

6. Her answering machine says: "Hello, this is Helen Mitchel's machine. Sorry I'm not home right now but if you leave a story, I'll call you back."

 ____

7. This afternoon she went shopping. In the first three shops she just looked at but in the last shop she bought a book.

 ____

8. When she came home, her friend called on the phone and said: "Good afternoon Mrs. Mitchel, what's up?"

 ____

9. Later that evening she went to the living room, sat down in the shower and watched TV.

 ____

points: 9 *1 point for each mistake*

2

Using words from the two boxes below, you can build 15 words which have been used in this chapter. Be careful: some of them are spelled in one word, and others are spelled in two words!

hang look call super microwave answering try gift living look cup shop dish hold department	assistant on around room shop board washer for machine oven on back store market on

______________ ______________

______________ ______________

______________ ______________

______________ ______________

______________ ______________

______________ ______________

______________ ______________

____

1 point for each word points: 15

0–12 points ☹	14–19 points 😐	20–24 points ☺
Too many mistakes – read this chapter again!	That was OK, but you can do better!	You did a really good job!

maximum number of points: 24

Geheimtipps zum Vokabellernen

Hast du in diesem Kapitel Wörter entdeckt, die du dir überhaupt nicht merken kannst? Versuch es mal mit diesen Geheimtipps. Sie verraten dir, wie du dir Wörter merken kannst, von denen du dachtest, das wird nie etwas.

1. Das Hasswort

Erkläre dem Wort: „Ich hasse dich. Dich werde ich mir nie merken." Du kannst es auch anschreien. Wiederhole das dreimal und du wirst dich sicher daran erinnern.

2. Das Deckenwort

Hänge einen Zettel mit einem oder zwei schwierigen Wörtern an die Decke über die Tür zu deinem (Klassen-)Zimmer und nimm dir vor, nie dorthin zu sehen. Du wirst feststellen, dass du dir das Wort nach kurzer Zeit merkst.

3. Die Geschichte

Nimm alle Wörter einer Lektion, die du dir nicht merken kannst, und erzähle eine Geschichte damit. Sie kann auch auf Deutsch sein, wichtig ist nur, dass die englischen Wörter auf Englisch eingefügt werden. Die Geschichte muss übrigens keinen Sinn ergeben.

4. Der Spickzettel

Schreibe dir vor dem Vokabeltest oder der Klassenarbeit einen Spickzettel mit den Wörtern, die du dir nicht merken kannst. Stecke ihn dann in der Stunde vor dem Test in deinen Schuh. So hast du ihn dabei und wirst ihn mit Sicherheit nicht verwenden (du kannst es vorher auch deiner Lehrerin/deinem Lehrer sagen). Du wirst sehen: er hilft trotzdem.

Was ich bereits kann ...

Kreuze an, was für dich zutrifft.

	Kein Problem	Hier mache ich noch Fehler	Muss ich unbedingt noch üben
6 Präpositionen und phrasal verbs			
1. Ich weiß, was eine Präposition ist.			
2. Ich kenne mindestens fünf Präpositionen der Zeit und des Ortes und kann sie anwenden.			
3. Ich kenne mindestens fünf Präpositionen, die sowohl Ort als auch Zeit bezeichnen können.			
4. Ich kenne mindestens neun *phrasal verbs* und kann sie in Sätzen anwenden.			
7 Konjunktionen			
5. Ich kenne mindestens sechs Konjunktionen und kann sie richtig im Satz anwenden.			
6. Ich erkenne, wenn in einem Satz eine falsche Konjunktion verwendet wurde.			
7. Ich kann in manchen Fällen die Bedeutung eines Satzes deutlich verändern, indem ich die Konjunktion durch eine andere ersetze.			
8 Tipps zum Lernen von Vokabeln			
8. Ich kenne das Wortfeld *At home*.			
9. Ich kenne das Wortfeld *On the telephone*.			
10. Ich kenne das Wortfeld *At the shops*.			
11. Ich kenne verschiedene Strategien, neues Vokabular zu lernen.			

Englisch verstehen

Hier trainierst du

- einen geschriebenen, englischen Text zu verstehen und
- einen gesprochenen, englischen Text zu verstehen.
  Nutze dazu die Audio-CD.

9 Leseverstehen: Einen geschriebenen Text verstehen

22/4/06

Some boys at my school always make fun of my friend and call her fat, which she isn't at all. She isn't super skinny like a super model but she's not fat either – the things they say really hurt her. How can I help her? What can I say to make her feel better?

Sarah

From: Girl, 04/2006, p. 22

1 Check-up

Tick the correct answer.

1. Sarah's friend is
   - ☐ happy at school.
   - ☐ unhappy at school.
   - ☐ happy at home.
   - ☐ unhappy at home.

2. Sarah wrote this letter to
   - ☐ a friend.
   - ☐ her parents.
   - ☒ a youth magazine.
   - ☐ a teacher.

3. If someone is "skinny" it means that he / she is
   - ☐ happy.
   - ☐ fat.
   - ☐ hungry.
   - ☐ thin.

4. Sarah wrote this letter in
   - ☐ January.
   - ☒ April.
   - ☐ August.
   - ☐ December.

Einen geschriebenen Text verstehen

Wie oft ist es dir schon passiert, dass du in der Schule, im Internet oder anderswo auf einen englischsprachigen Text gestoßen bist und gedacht hast: **„Oh je, da verstehe ich ja kein Wort?"** Als nächstes hast du dann wahrscheinlich den Text weggeklickt oder hast im Unterricht abgeschaltet. Das ist aber überhaupt nicht nötig, wenn du dich an einige **einfache Regeln** hältst, die das Lesen von Texten vereinfachen.

Beim ersten Lesen

Versuche **auf keinen Fall**, alles auf einmal zu verstehen, sondern versuche zunächst nur zu verstehen, wovon der Text handelt ***(reading for gist)***.

Achte dabei auf:
1. Überschriften,
2. Fettgedrucktes,
3. Bilder,
4. den ersten und den letzten Satz des Textes.

Kümmere dich auf **keinen Fall um unbekannte Wörter**, lies einfach weiter.
Nach diesem Durchgang kannst du entscheiden, ob dieser Text für dich interessant genug ist, um ihn genauer zu lesen.

Beim zweiten Lesen

Jetzt kannst du den Text auf **genauere Informationen** hin untersuchen ***(reading for detail)***. In der Schule hast du dazu wahrscheinlich eine Aufgabe von deinem Lehrer erhalten (z.B. *Find reasons why Linda is happy after she has met George.*). Wenn du den Text dagegen für dich liest, suchst du nach dem, was dich interessiert.

Dabei solltest du auf Folgendes achten:
1. Lies immer mit einem **Stift in der Hand**. Du kannst dann Wichtiges (am besten Stichwörter) unterstreichen und Ausrufezeichen oder Fragezeichen an den Rand schreiben.
2. **Unterstreiche Wörter, die du nicht verstehst**. Du kannst versuchen, ihre Bedeutung zu erschließen ***(guessing)***, oder du kannst sie im Lexikon nachschlagen.

Aufschreiben der Ergebnisse

Nach dem zweiten Lesen solltest du den Text noch einmal durchgehen und die wichtigen Informationen geordnet aufschreiben (dabei helfen dir natürlich deine Unterstreichungen und Notizen). In der Schule macht ihr das meistens gemeinsam an der Tafel, zu Hause bist du auf dich alleine gestellt.

Tipps zum Umgang mit unbekanntem Vokabular

Besonders wichtig beim Lesen ist das **Verstehen unbekannter Wörter**. Hier einige Tipps, die dir helfen können, mit fremdem Vokabular umzugehen:
Zuerst musst du entscheiden, ob du das Wort überhaupt verstehen musst. Viele Wörter sind für das Verständnis des gesamten Textes völlig unwichtig. Mache dir die Mühe, einzelne Wörter zu erraten oder nachzuschlagen also nur da, wo es sich lohnt! Wenn das der Fall ist, kannst du das Raten mit ein paar Tricks unterstützen.

1. Das englische Wort ähnelt einem deutschen, z. B. *fish*.
2. Bei zusammengesetzten Wörtern kennst du oft eines der Wörter oder sogar beide und kannst so das ganze erschließen:
   starfish (*star*, Stern + *fish*, Fisch = Seestern).
3. Vielleicht kennst du ein Wort aus der gleichen Wortfamilie:
   a fish, to fish.
4. Vielleicht kennst du ein ähnliches Wort in einer anderen Sprache: engl. *pardon*, franz. *pardon* (Entschuldigung).
5. Oft bleibt dir aber nur übrig, das Wort aus dem Zusammenhang zu erschließen. In einem Text über Angler, in dem der Satz *He was excited because he had a big fish on his hook.* vorkommt, muss *hook* entweder Angel oder Haken heißen. In der Tat heißt es Haken, aber auch wenn du Angel vermutet hättest, hättest du verstanden, worum es geht!

9.1 Bullying at schools: an everyday problem!

2

Read the following text for gist and then answer the questions below by ticking the correct answers (sometimes more than one answer is possible).

Bullying at schools: an everyday problem!

More and more pupils feel bullied at school. Bullies call other pupils names, they tell lies about their victims, steal from them, or even attack them. Last year two-thirds of all pupils in the U.K. said that they had been bullied in some form during the school year.

Why do bullies bully?

Psychologists say that most bullies have problems themselves. They feel unsure about themselves because they might have trouble at home or at school. They may also feel alone and think they will find friends by making fun of other people. Often they even want to be like the person they bully. They are jealous and therefore they attack.

Who are the victims?

The people who are bullied, the victims, are often people who show that they are weak because it's much easier to attack a weak person than a strong one. Often the victims look different from other people (slim, overweight, strange clothes), or they are not good at certain things (often sports), or they may not have many friends. Any kind of weakness attracts bullies.

Help

If you need help because someone bullies you, call the Bully-Line: 944-3454.

Questions

1. This text is about
   - ☐ how to make friends at school.
   - ☐ a big problem that can be found at many schools.
   - ☐ pupils who get bad marks.

2. A bully is someone
   - ☐ who is friendly to everybody.
   - ☐ who usually has got a problem.
   - ☐ who is not nice to other people.

3. The text says that last year
   - [ ] many pupils had problems with bullies.
   - [ ] just a few pupils had problems with bullies.
   - [ ] almost no pupils had problems with bullies.

4. The text wants to help
   - [ ] bullies.
   - [ ] people who are bullied.
   - [ ] people who want to know more about bullies.

3

Read the text again for detail.

1. Take a pen and underline the information you need to help you answer the questions below.
2. Also underline any words you don't understand using a different colour.

Questions:
1. What do bullies do?
2. Why do they do it?
3. Who are their victims?

4

Here's a list of words you might not have understood. Guess their meaning.

Word	Meaning
to call s.o. names	
victim	
psychologist	
unsure	
overweight	
weakness	

5

Sum up what you found out. Complete the diagram.

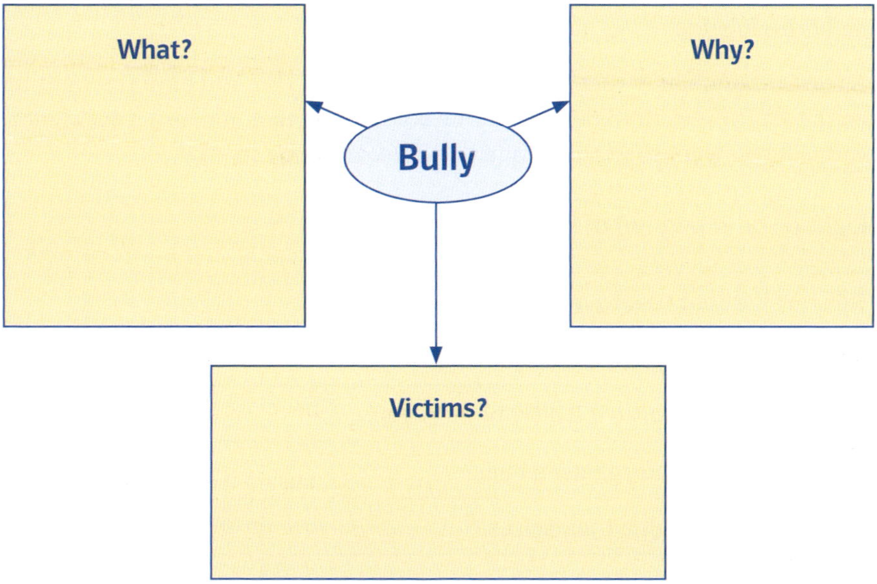

9.2 What can you do against bullies?

6

Read the following text for gist and then answer the questions below by ticking the correct answers.

What can you do against bullies?

There are **many things you can do** if someone tries to bully you. Maybe you will have to try different methods until you succeed.

The first approach is to **ignore the bully**. If he calls you names, don't react! Bullies often get bored if their victim does not seem to be hurt by their attacks. The next step must be to get your **friends to help** you. They can help you by just being with you while you are at school, for example. Bullies like to bother pupils who are alone, because it's easier. Your friends can also defend you against the bully. If a bully sees that your friends help you and don't leave you alone, he will usually back off. If you can't ignore the bully because you are really hurt or you don't have enough friends to help you, **talk to adults** about it. That could be your parents, or a teacher, or anyone else you think might be able to help you.

Never hit a bully. That usually makes things worse and might get you into trouble yourself. However, **never run away** from them or show them that they hurt your feelings. If you do that, you can be sure that the bully will go on bothering you.

Always remember: it's the bully who is wrong, not you! You have the right to be the way you want to be. If the bully doesn't like that, it's his problem, not yours. If you want to win against a bully **you must be strong!**

Right (r) or wrong (w) or not in the text (nit)?	r	w	nit
This text is about how to react to a bully.			
There is not much you can do against a bully.			
It's OK to call the police if a bully bothers you.			
Friends can help you against a bully.			
Bullies often are alone themselves.			
It doesn't help to hit a bully.			

7

Read the text again for detail.

1. Take a pen and underline the information you think is important.
2. Also underline the words you don't understand using a different colour.

8

Find and underline the mistakes in the following statements.

1. If someone bullies you, you should first ignore the bully and then ask your friends for help. If that doesn't help, catch the bully on his way home and give him a good beating.
2. Bullies like to bully people who are alone. That's why you should try not to be alone when "your" bully is around. Always ask a friend to come with you. If you don't have friends, just run away when you see the bully, that way he can't bother you.
3. It is your fault if a bully picks on you. So if the bully says that your clothes are stupid, buy new clothes and the problem will be solved. If that doesn't work, talk to adults who might be able to help you.

9

Here's a list of words which you might not have understood. Guess their meaning. If you don't think it is important to know exactly what the word means, write down (in German) that it means something like …

Word	Meaning	Not so important, means something like
method		
to succeed		
approach		
to ignore		
to bother		
to back off		

10

Sum up what you found out. Complete the table. A table is useful if you want to compare two different ideas about the same subject.

Dos and Don'ts when you are bullied

Dos (what you should do)	Don'ts (what you shouldn't do)
______________________	______________________
______________________	______________________
______________________	______________________
______________________	______________________
______________________	______________________
______________________	______________________

I must always be ______________.

9.3 Suzie's experience with a bully

11

Read the following text for gist and then complete the sentences below.

Suzie's experience with a bully

There was a bully (who I barely even knew, so she had no reason to start being mean to me) who just recently started giving me trouble. I mean, she just called me names and tried to embarrass me in front of the whole class. I just totally ignored her, remained strong, and when she tried to bully me right in front of boys she likes, they saw that she was stupid and I was nice! Suddenly her friends started to like me and feel sorry for me and didn't like her any more. THAT made her so incredibly angry and jealous! And that, my friends, was sweet victory. She soon gave up and I had a lot of new friends.

The best thing to remember here, people, is that your bully feeds on how bad he/she makes you feel. This is a sign that that person is insecure and immature! Be strong out there, and you'll win more friends. This is something that will give you a happier, easier life, now and in the future.

Suzie

Suzie was bullied by …
- ☐ a boy.
- ☐ a girl.

She …
- ☐ hit the bully.
- ☐ ignored the bully.
- ☐ asked her teacher for help.

Now she …
- ☐ has a lot of new friends.
- ☐ is alone because her friends left her.
- ☐ doesn't go to school any more because she is afraid.

12

Read the text again for detail.

1. Take a pen and underline the information you think is important.
2. Also underline the words you don't understand using a different colour.

13

Complete the sentences in the following summary, using the information from Suzie's letter. A summary is useful for collecting the information you need in a few words.

One day a _______________ started bullying Suzie. That was very strange because Suzie didn't _______________ her very well. But Suzie just _______________ the bully and remained _______________. Suzie really won the conflict when the bully tried to bother Suzie _______________ her friends. The bully's friends didn't react like she had hoped they would. They saw that the bully was _______________ and Suzie was _______________. So the bully lost her _______________ and Suzie had _______________ new friends. Suzie believes that the most important thing to know about bullies is that they like it when they see that their victim feels _______________. That's why it is important to stay _______________.

14

Here's a list of words you might not have understood. Guess their meaning. If you don't think it is important to know exactly what the word means, write down (in German) that it means something like …

Word	Meaning	Not so important, means something like
barely		
to embarrass		
to remain		
to feed		

15

Sum up what you found out.

Fill in the gaps in the flow chart. A flow chart is a good way of showing how one thing happens after another.

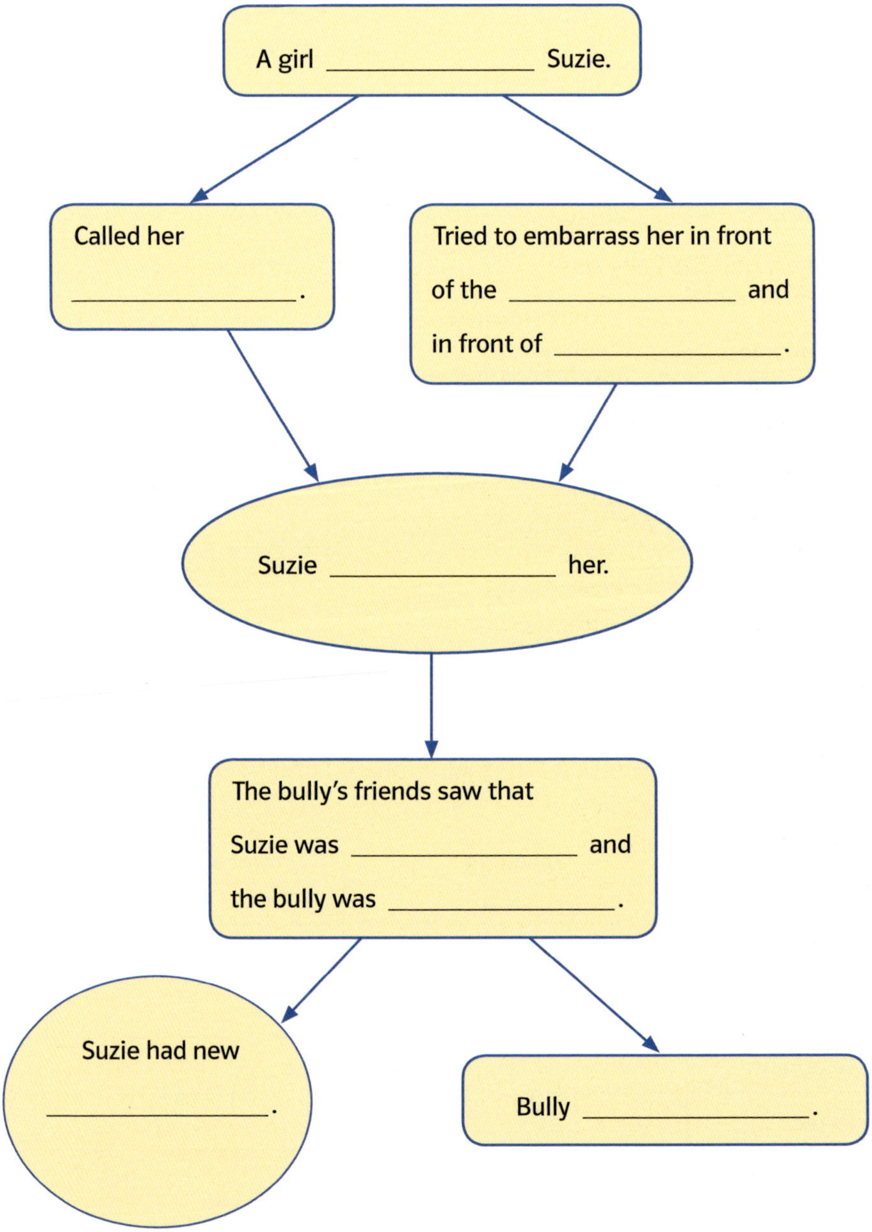

Statt einen Test zu schreiben, beurteilst du deine Kenntnisse im Bereich Leseverstehen am besten selbst. Denke über die sechs Aussagen nach und kreuze dann erst an.

Aussage	Klappt sehr gut	Gelingt mir manchmal	Muss ich weiter üben
Ich kann beim ersten Lesen eines englischen Textes verstehen, worum es grundsätzlich geht.			
Ich kann beim zweiten Lesen erkennen, welche unbekannten Wörter für mich wichtig sind und welche nicht.			
Ich kann die wichtigen unbekannten Wörter erschließen, ohne in einem Lexikon nachzuschlagen.			
Ich kann beim zweiten Lesen die für mich wichtigen Schlüsselwörter und -sätze herausfinden und unterstreichen.			
Ich kann mit Hilfe meiner Unterstreichungen gezielte Fragen zum Text beantworten.			
Ich kann die wichtigen Aussagen und Fakten eines Textes in Tabellen, Mindmaps oder *flow charts* richtig eintragen.			

10 Hörverstehen: Einen gesprochenen Text verstehen

1 Check-up 19

You will hear different sounds taken from the everyday life of an English police officer. Tick the correct sound.

1.
- ☐ a) a telephone is ringing
- ☐ b) a doorbell is ringing
- ☐ c) an alarm clock is going off

2.
- ☐ a) an ambulance is driving by
- ☐ b) a police car is driving by
- ☐ c) a firetruck is driving by

3.
- ☐ a) a woman is crying for help
- ☐ b) a man is crying for help
- ☐ c) a group of people are crying for help

4.
- ☐ a) two cars are crashing into each other
- ☐ b) two bicycles are crashing into each other
- ☐ c) somebody is being hit by a car

Hörverstehen

55 % der Zeit, die ein Mensch wach ist, verbringt er damit zu hören und zu versuchen, das Gehörte zu verstehen. Deshalb ist es besonders wichtig, diese Fähigkeit auch in der Fremdsprache zu üben.

Hörverstehen heißt aber vieles:
1. Zunächst musst du natürlich die **Worte** verstehen.
2. **Geräusche** helfen dir oft dabei, eine Situation zu erkennen und erleichtern so das Verständnis des Gesagten.
3. **Kultur:** Wahrscheinlich konntest du z. B. die zweite Frage des **Check-up** nicht beantworten, da du die Unterschiede zwischen den Sirenen englischer Krankenwagen, Feuerwehrautos und Polizeiautos nicht kennst.

4. **Du hörst das, was dich interessiert:** Bei einer Ansage auf dem Bahnhof hörst du z. B. nur so lange zu, bis du weißt, ob dein Zug betroffen ist, bei einem Telefongespräch mit deiner besten Freundin / deinem besten Freund aber hörst du genauer hin, da du auch antworten willst.
   Umgekehrt bedeutet das jedoch: Verstehst du ein Wort nicht, kennst du das Thema nicht, über das gesprochen wird, oder sind die Geräusche so laut, dass du nicht hören kannst, was gesagt wird, verstehst du vielleicht nur noch „Bahnhof".

Das folgende Kapitel, in dem Inspektor Atkinson einen Kriminalfall aufklären soll, hilft dir dabei, Strategien zu entwickeln, diese Probleme zu meistern. Je nachdem, was du erfahren/wissen/herausbekommen möchtest, ist es sinnvoll einen Text einmal oder öfter anzuhören. Grundsätzlich solltest du auf Folgendes achten.

Beim ersten Hören

1. ***Identify the situation:*** Es ist immer gut zu wissen, worum es in einem Gespräch geht oder auch wo es stattfindet und wer spricht.
2. ***Listen for gist:*** Meist solltest du zuerst das Große und Ganze ***(the gist)*** verstehen.
3. ***Guess intelligently:*** Oft wird man durch Nebengeräusche gestört, oder man versteht einzelne Worte nicht. Dann ist die erste Regel: ***Don't panic!*** Man kann die „Lücken" oft durch cleveres Nachdenken und Raten schließen oder man erkennt schnell, dass die Worte für das eigene Textverständnis nicht wichtig sind.

Beim zweiten oder dritten Hören

4. Fortführen des ***intelligent guessing***.
5. ***Listen for detail:*** Nach Einzelheiten sucht man immer erst beim zweiten Hören. Oft schreibt man diese dann auch auf ***(taking notes)***. Wichtig hierbei ist, dass man nur Stichworte ***(key words)*** aufschreibt, da für ganze Sätze während des Zuhörens normalerweise keine Zeit ist.

10.1 Die Situation erkennen

2 20

Listen to the situations once and tick the correct answer.

A morning in inspector Atkinson's life

1.

☐ a) Inspector Atkinson's radio alarm wakes her up in the morning.

☐ b) Inspector Atkinson is listening to her radio in the car.

☐ c) Inspector Atkinson is at the radio shop to buy a new stereo.

2.

☐ a) The people are happy because they don't have to pay today.

☐ b) The people are angry because the bus is late.

☐ c) The people are angry because the underground is late.

3.

☐ a) Mrs. Atkinson is buying some coffee for breakfast.

☐ b) Mrs. Atkinson is buying a newspaper.

☐ c) Mrs. Atkinson is buying pizza for lunch.

4.

☐ a) Mrs. Atkinson is sitting in her office.

☐ b) Mrs. Atkinson is having breakfast in the police cafeteria.

☐ c) Mrs. Atkinson is doing the washing-up at home.

10.2 Den Sinn verstehen

3 21

Listen to this text just once and tick the correct answers:
r = right, w = wrong, nit = not in text

Mrs. Atkinson meets her colleague*, Mr. Mitchum, in her office.
Here are a few words you might need to know before you listen to the text:

murder – Mord; **murderer** – Mörder; **case** – hier: (Kriminal)Fall; **witness** – Zeuge/Zeugin; **gun** – Gewehr

	r	w	nit
Inspector Atkinson is having a great morning.			
She dreamed about a great birthday party last night.			
Mr. Mitchum dreamed about a murder last night.			
Something terrible happened in Bold Street last night.			
Mr. MacAllister was a millionaire.			
An old man saw everything and called the police.			
Inspector Atkinson is going to call the old man right away.			

***colleague** – someone who works with you in the same place

10.3 Die Einzelheiten heraushören

4 22

Listen to this text twice and decide who it is that Mr. Maple is describing. Tick the correct answers.

Inspector Atkinson is talking to Mr. Maple. She wants to know what the two men Mr. Maple saw last night looked like.
She has pictures of six criminals who have just done their time in prison.

☐ Longknife Jane

☐ Revolver Andy

☐ Robin Shoot

☐ Monster Martha

☐ Getaway Bill

☐ Killer Joe

5 23

Listen to this text twice, and find and mark the places on the map.

Inspector Atkinson is going to visit the two people Mr. Maple saw last night. Mr. Mitchum tells her where they live. Of course you start at Scotland Yard!

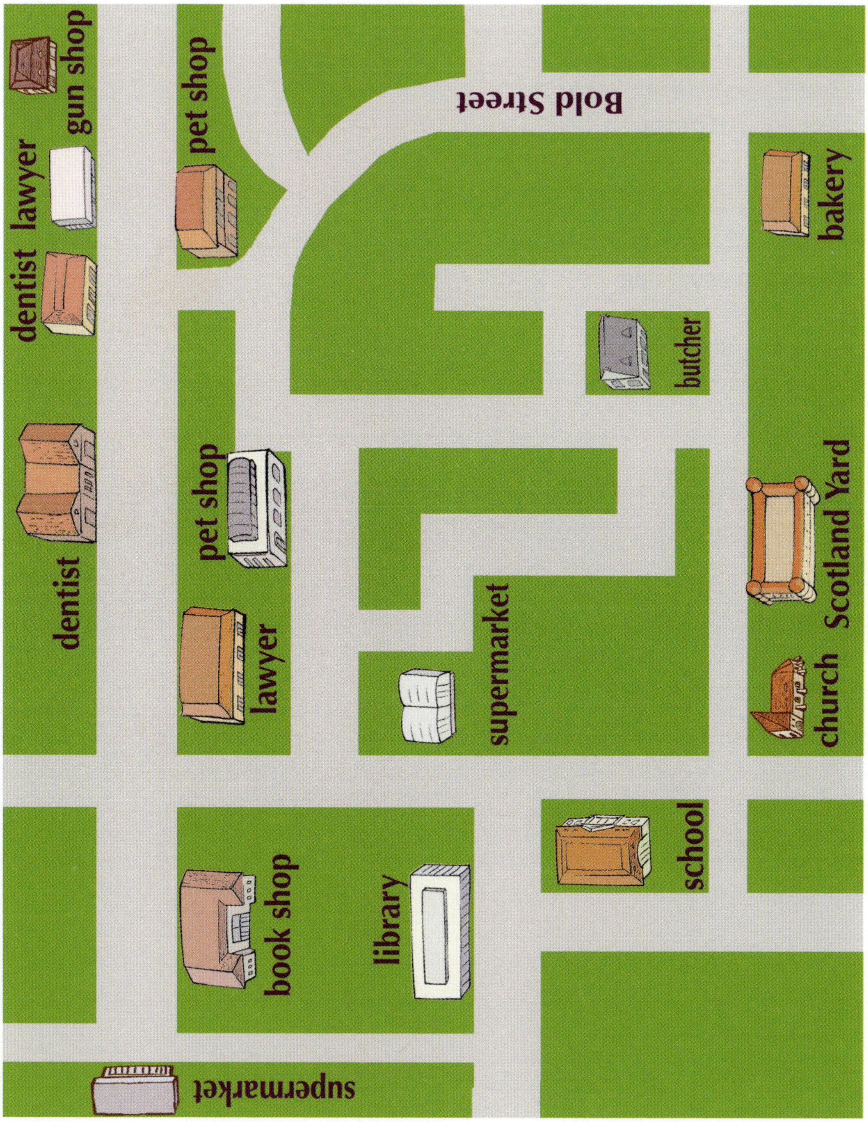

6 24–25

Listen to these two texts twice, or more often if necessary. Take notes – they will help you to answer the questions.

Inspector Atkinson goes to pay a visit to the two suspects. First she talks to Killer Joe, then to Revolver Andy. To make sure that she won't forget anything, she has written down the questions she wants to ask them.

Question	Suspect No. 1	Suspect No. 2
What have you been doing since you left prison?		
What were you doing last night at 2 o'clock in the morning?		
Do you know where Bold Street is?		
If "yes": Did you see or hear anything strange there last night?		
Do you own a gun?		
Do you know Andrew MacAllister?		

7

Tick the correct answers.

Why does Inspector Atkinson think that Revolver Andy is the murderer? There were five hints in this chapter.

1. The name "Revolver Andy" shows that he is a bad man. ☐
2. Two people say they saw a man who looked like Revolver Andy in Bold Street last night, but Revolver Andy says he wasn't there. ☐
3. People who wear dark coats and hats are always suspicious*. ☐
4. Revolver Andy could easily hide the gun under his coat, but Killer Joe couldn't. He was wearing shorts and a T-shirt. ☐
5. Revolver Andy works in a gun-shop. It was easy for him to take a gun from the shop and kill Andrew MacAllister. ☐
6. Revolver Andy has no witnesses to back up his story that he was sleeping last night. Killer Joe was seen by Mr. Maple. ☐
7. Revolver Andy knows Andrew MacAllister and doesn't like him, because MacAllister likes Andy's girlfriend. ☐
8. Revolver Andy talks about MacAllister in the simple past tense, although Inspector Atkinson hasn't told him that he was killed. ☐
9. Revolver Andy is not friendly to Mrs. Atkinson. Killer Joe is much nicer. ☐

*__suspicious__ – verdächtig

Statt einen Test zu schreiben, beurteilst du deine Kenntnisse im Bereich Hörverstehen am besten selbst. Denke über die sechs Aussagen nach und kreuze dann erst an.

Aussage	**Klappt sehr gut**	**Gelingt mir manchmal**	**Muss ich weiter üben**
Ich kann die Situationen aufgrund von Geräuschen und wichtigen Äußerungen erkennen.			
Ich kann nach einmaligem Hören Hauptaussagen eines Dialoges verstehen.			
Ich kann Wichtiges von Unwichtigem nach einmaligem Hören unterscheiden.			
Ich kann gezielt Details aus einem Text heraushören.			
Ich kann mir beim zweiten oder dritten Hören wichtige Details in Stichwörtern während des Hörens notieren.			
Worte, die ich nicht kenne, werfen mich nicht aus der Bahn. Ich kann sie erschließen oder erkenne, dass sie für mich nicht wichtig sind.			

Was ich bereits kann ...

Kreuze an, was für dich zutrifft.

	Kein Problem	Hier mache ich noch Fehler	Muss ich unbedingt noch üben
9 Leseverstehen: Einen geschriebenen Text verstehen			
1. Ich verstehe einen englischen Text beim ersten Lesen so, dass ich weiß, worum es darin geht.			
2. Ich kenne Techniken und Strategien, wie ich mir einen geschriebenen Text durch weiteres Lesen erschließen kann.			
10 Hörverstehen: Einen gesprochenen Text verstehen			
3. Ich verstehe einen gesprochenen Text beim ersten Hören so, dass ich weiß, worum es darin geht.			
4. Ich kenne Techniken und Strategien, wie ich mir einen gesprochenen Text durch weiteres Hören erschließen kann.			
5. Ich gerate nicht in Panik, wenn ich gesprochene oder geschriebene Wörter nicht sofort verstehe, sondern kann diese mit bestimmten Techniken erschließen oder erraten.			

Lösungen

1 Bedingungssätze

1 Check-up

1. If we go to Scotland, I will spend a day at Loch Ness.
2. If we go to Liverpool, we must watch a football game.
3. If we go to the Isle of Wight, we can go swimming.
4. If we go to Wales, we can climb Mount Snowdon.
5. If we go to Northern Ireland, we can spend a few days in Belfast.
6. If we go to South England, we must go swimming / visit Stonehenge.
7. If we go to Nottingham, I will take a walk in Sherwood Forest

Can, *will* und *must* sind frei austauschbar.

2

1. *Mrs. Smith:* If Liverpool loses again, you will be grumpy.
2. *Susan:* If we don't go swimming on the Isle of Wight, I will be very angry.
3. *Max:* If we spend time at the beach, I will build a lot of sand castles.
4. *Mrs. Smith:* If we visit Stonehenge, you will learn a lot about history.
5. *Mr. Smith:* If we climb Mount Snowdon, we will see very far.
6. *Max:* If we don't camp at Loch Ness, I will not see the monster.
7. *Susan:* If we spend a lot of time on camping grounds, I will make many new friends.
8. *Mrs. Smith:* If we go for a walk in Sherwood Forest, I will think of Robin Hood and his gang.

3

1. *Mrs. Smith:* You will be grumpy if Liverpool loses again.
2. *Susan:* I will be very angry if we don't go swimming on the Isle of Wight.
3. *Max:* I will build a lot of sand castles if we spend time at the beach.
4. *Mrs. Smith:* You will learn a lot about history if we visit Stonehenge.
5. *Mr. Smith:* We will see very far if we climb Mount Snowdon.
6. *Max:* I will not see the monster if we don't camp at Loch Ness.
7. *Susan:* I will make many new friends if we spend a lot of time on camping grounds.
8. *Mrs. Smith:* I will think of Robin Hood and his gang if we go for a walk in Sherwood Forest.

4

1. if 2. if 3. when 4. when 5. if 6. when 7. if 8. if 9. when

5 Check-up

1. *Mr. Smith:* If I had a lot of money, I would rent a VIP-lounge in Liverpool.
2. *Susan:* If I had a lot of money, I would travel to New York.
3. *Max:* If I had a lot of money, I would fly to the moon.

6

1. If Max was old enough to drive a car, he would drive to Loch Ness with it.
2. If Susan had a plane, she would fly to America.
3. If Mrs. Smith was able to travel in time, she would meet Robin Hood.
4. If Mr. Smith were a millionaire, he would go to the Football World Championships.

7

Der Einsatz verschiedener modaler Hilfsverben verändert natürlich die Bedeutung der Sätze.

Max:

If I took a picture of Nessie, I would be a star / might be rich.

Susan:

If I met a star in Manhattan, he might take me to a fancy disco.

If I spent a week in Manhattan, I would/could/might climb to the top of the Empire State Building.

Mrs. Smith:

If I found Robin Hood, I would/could/might help him to kill the Sheriff of Nottingham.

If I killed the Sheriff of Nottingham, the police might/would/could arrest me. (I would be a star.)

Mr. Smith:

If I went to the Football World Championships, I would/could/might take my best friend with me.

If we met the British team, we would/could/might invite them for dinner.

8 1

1. might see / will see 2. were 3. would be 4. believe 5. won't see 6. went 7. would meet / could meet / might meet 8. could lie 9. will show 10. will climb 11. were

Test

1

1. when 2. if 3. if 4. if 5. when 6. when

2

	Type I	Type II
If Mrs. Smith finds a job soon, the Smiths will go to America next year.	▯	☐
Susan would be very excited if they went there.	☐	▯
Max said: "I will only go if there are monsters in America."	▯	☐
Then Susan said: "If we found a monster, it would probably be King Kong."	☐	▯
If they go there, Mrs. Smith will read a lot of books about American history.	▯	☐

3

1. I will stay at home.
2. if we have enough money.
3. we could win a lot of money.
4. if you were quiet.
5. if he had a nice sister.
6. if we go to Scotland.
7. Nessie will come and kiss me.

Gerundium und Infinitiv 2

1 Check-up

What are their jobs?

I love my job …	I hate driving …	I love making a lot of …
He's a **vet.**	He's a **bus driver.**	She's a **manager.**

2 2

Alice: I love meeting friends. That's the best, because you can talk and have fun.

Andrew: That's right, especially if they like doing the same things as I do.

Fiona: I agree, but I think reading is great, too, because I can do that at home in my room when I'm alone.

Alex: Bah, I'm tired of reading. We have to read at school all the time. I'm good at doing sports and I'm excellent at playing football. Those are my hobbies.

Tim: I think doing sports is OK, but I'm terrible at playing football. I prefer skiing, it's a lot of fun and I'm good at it.

Sarah: I think that going shopping is also a great hobby. I love looking at new books and clothes in the shops. I only wish I had more money.

Kirk: I disagree, shopping is terrible. Listening to music is so much more fun. I'm also interested in finding out about pop and rock groups, so I also enjoy reading magazines about the music scene.

Gerund used as subject	**Gerund used as object**	**Gerund used after adj. + prep.**
– reading is great – doing sports is OK – going shopping is also a great hobby – shopping is terrible – Listening to music is so much more fun	– I love meeting friends – they like doing the same things as I do – I prefer skiing – I love looking at new books and clothes – I also enjoy reading magazines	– I'm tired of reading – I'm good at doing sports – I'm excellent at playing football – I'm terrible at playing football – I'm also interested in finding out about pop and rock groups

3

1. John loves **reading comics**.
2. Alice enjoys **playing football**.
3. Sarah hates **skiing**.
4. Abdul doesn't like **running**.
5. Philip likes **watching TV**.

4

Die Antworten können unterschiedlich sein. Die Satzstruktur bleibt jedoch die gleiche.

Mr. Hunt: Cooking is terrible.
Mrs. Giggs: Lying on the beach is not much fun at all.
Mr. Miller: Working in the garden is great.
Mrs. Hathaway: Reading books is the best. / Reading books is what I like doing best.
Mr. Singh: Singing is terrible.
Mrs. Bangs: Going for a walk with my dog is very relaxing.
Mr. Smith: Reading newspapers is a lot of fun.
Mrs. Sander: Writing letters is the worst. / Writing letters is the worst way to spend time.

5 3

Philip: My dad is very chaotic. So he is terrible at (not very good at) keeping things in order.
Hilary: My mother is a French teacher. She is good at teaching French but I'm sure she would be terrible (not very good) at teaching Maths.
Alex: My brother is so slow. So he is not very good (terrible) at running, but he is good at playing chess.
Sarah: You know, my little sister is really interested in (good at) cooking. That's why she got five cook books for her birthday.
Abdul: My brother is just as tired of doing sports as I am. He says it makes him hot, thirsty and tired. Sports are terrible.

6 Check-up

1. My mother doesn't allow me to listen to loud music.
2. She always tells me to go to bed early.
3. It's really difficult to do homework when the weather is nice.
4. I think it's wrong to tell children what to do.
5. My mother hates to be strict with me.

7

Hier sind natürlich auch andere Lösungen denkbar. Wichtig ist, dass du alle Satzteile aus der vierten Spalte verwendet hast.

1. My parents always tell me to clean up my room.
2. Our teachers always ask me to do my homework.
3. My friends sometimes ask me to help them with their homework.
4. Our teachers never order me to leave the room.
5. My parents sometimes allow me to stay out late in the evening.
6. My parents often allow me to go to parties.
7. My parents never order me to work in the garden.
8. Our teachers sometimes tell us to clean up the playground.
9. I think it's difficult to be a pop star.
10. I believe it's not right to order pupils to clean the playground.
11. I don't think it's easy to earn a lot of money.
12. I think it's not right to hit your friends.
13. I think it's difficult to be nice to somebody I don't like.
14. I'm sure it's hard to tell teenagers when to be home in the evening.

8

1. Cleaning the house is great.	☒
To clean the house is great.	☐
2. I hate to do extra work for school.	☒
I hate doing extra work for school.	☒
3. My father is excellent at cooking.	☒
My father is excellent at to cook.	☐
4. Yesterday my class began to do a new project on hobbies.	☒
Yesterday my class began doing a new project on hobbies.	☒
5. My friends and I believe it's wrong to send teenagers to school.	☒
My friends and I believe it's wrong sending teenagers to school.	☐
6. I really love to do homework.	☒
I really love doing homework.	☒
7. I hope my parents will allow me to buy a new CD tomorrow.	☒
I hope my parents will allow me buying a new CD tomorrow.	☐
8. If I continue getting good marks, my parents will buy me a present.	☒
If I continue to get good marks, my parents will buy me a present.	☒
9. My best friend really enjoys to eat a lot.	☐
My best friend really enjoys eating a lot.	☒

9

1. *Ich bin sicher, dass er nicht vergessen wird dich anzurufen.*
   I'm sure he won't forget to phone you. ☒
   I'm sure he won't forget phoning you. ☐
2. *Ich habe vergessen, dass ich das Buch gekauft habe.*
   I don't remember to buy the book. ☐
   I don't remember buying the book. ☒
3. *Ich werde sicherlich daran denken, dir eine Postkarte zu schicken.*
   I'm sure I will remember sending you a postcard. ☐
   I'm sure I will remember to send you a postcard. ☒
4. *Der Fahrer des Wagens hielt an, um aus dem Fenster zu schauen.*
   The driver of the car stopped looking out of the window. ☐
   The driver of the car stopped to look out of the window. ☒

Test

1

1. Yesterday my girlfriend asked me **to do** her homework on the bus.
2. It was really early in the morning and I'm terrible at doing homework so early.
3. So I said: "**Doing** homework on the bus is not right. You should do it at home."
4. She answered: "Stop **saying** such stupid things and help me!"
5. I told her **to leave** me alone and closed my eyes.
6. She started screaming at me and walked away.
7. Now I'm looking for a new girlfriend and I will make sure that she prefers **doing** her homework at home.

2

Infinitive sind unterstrichen, Gerundien blau hervorgehoben.

Hobbies and free time

Most teenagers **love having** as much free time as possible. They find it easy to spend day after day at home with their friends or they go outside and do sports or walk around town. Most of them **hate doing** homework although some like to do it, too. Often teenagers must ask their parents to allow them to go somewhere, especially in the evenings. Many parents find it difficult to say "no" when that happens, but they of course say it anyway. Most teenagers **are terrible at accepting** a "no" from their parents, and they start to argue with them. Usually, they both – teenagers and parents – **hate having** these discussions, and usually the parents win. But still, teenagers continue to fight for their freedom* and will never **stop doing** so. **Growing up** is a difficult time, but many parents would say that **being** a parent is almost as difficult, too.

***freedom** – Freiheit

3

1. Most teenagers love to have …
2. Most of them hate to do homework …
3. … although some like doing them, too.
4. … start arguing with them.
5. … hate to have these discussions …
6. … the teenagers continue fighting …

Das *present perfect simple* und *progressive* 3

1 Check-up

1. Some guests **have watched** TV.
2. People **have eaten** a lot of crisps.
3. An idiot **has painted** a red heart on the mirror.
4. The CD-player **has fallen** off the sideboard.
5. Many people **have left** their empty bottles on the floor.

2 Check-up 4

Mr. Smith: Oh hi. It's great to be home. Our trip was terrible. Look at the weather. It has been raining all day and we (1) **have been driving** for hours.

Mrs. Smith: Yes, it was awful, but I didn't mind because I was asleep until a minute ago. What (2) **have** you **been doing** all morning?

Andrew: Oh … well … err … … hm …

Alice: We (3) **have been watching** TV. There is a great show on. Do you want to watch with us?

3

ring – write – learn – see – drink – show – be – read – leave – cut – hear – feel – come – meet – eat

4

1. written 2. learned 3. cut 4. seen, shown, been, read 5. drunk 6. left
7. come, heard 8. met 9. rung 10. eaten, felt

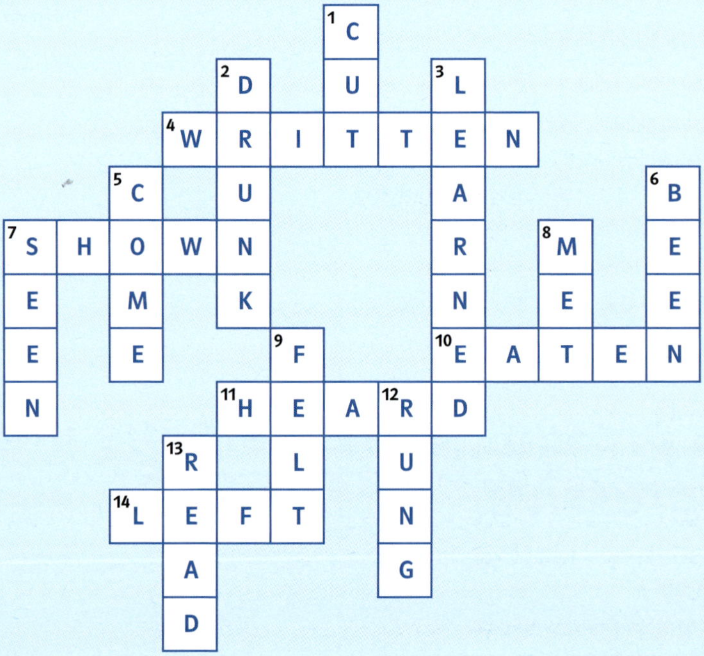

5 5

Talk before the party

Mary and Kate are getting ready for the party.

Mary: This will be a great evening, and Pete will be there, too. (1) **Have** you ever **met** him?

Kate: No I haven't. But we (2) **have written** emails to each other.

Mary: Oh really? That's nice. Do you know how old he is?

Kate: I think he (3) **has** just **turned** sixteen. His birthday was a week ago.

Mary: That's old. I thought he was younger. What about Billy? I (4) **haven't seen** him for weeks.

Kate: I met him last week. I think he will be there, but his girlfriend (5) **has** just **broken up** with him. I think her name was Donna.

Mary: Oh, that's good news. Now he's free again and he's only fourteen. That's a better age for us, isn't it? (6) **Have** you **bought/brought** that new make-up? I think we should use it today.

Kate: Oh no, it's not in my bag. I (7) **haven't brought** it. Well, maybe he'll like us anyway.

Mary: That's terrible, Kate! Why do you always forget important things? I (8) **have** never **met** anyone like you.

6 6

Party talk II

Kate: Wow, Alice, what a great party – and so many people!

Alice: Thank you Kate. We're very, very happy. The music is great, so people (1) **have been dancing** since the beginning.

Mary: How about Billy? Is he here?

Alice: Yes he is. He (2) **has been sitting** over there for two hours. I don't think he's very happy.

Kate: I'm not surprised. His girlfriend has just broken up with him. They (3) **have been going out** for two months.

Mary: That's a long time. I would be sad, too. Oh, hi Pete.

Pete: Hi, what (4) **have** you **been talking** about?

Kate: Oh, umm, the weather. Terrible, isn't it?

Pete: Yes, the sun (5) **hasn't been shining** for weeks now. Would you like to go outside anyway? I (6) **have been dancing** for an hour and need some fresh air.

Kate: Umm, of course. See you later, Mary.

7

Scenes from the party

1. They've been kissing for ten minutes.
2. He has eaten a pizza.
3. They've been talking since the party started.
4. They have painted a heart on the mirror.
5. He has just fallen asleep.
6. They've just met.
7. They've been standing in line for half an hour.

8 7

Talk after the party

1. for 2. since 3. for 4. since 5. for 6. since 7. for

Test

1

Preparing a party

1. They have written and sent out invitations.
2. They have bought (the) soft drinks.
3. They haven't put up posters.
4. They have made the food.
5. They haven't asked (their) friends for help.

2

1. I have been talking to Billy.
2. I have been buying make-up.
3. I have been shouting at Maria.
4. I have been screaming at Steve.
5. I have been thinking of my girlfriend.

3 8

Giving a party is not always fun!

Alice: Andrew, could you please get up and help me? You (1) **haven't been doing** anything (2) **for** three hours and the party starts in half an hour.

Andrew: That's not true. I (3) **have been thinking** about all the things that we must still do. It's terrible, I (4) **haven't worked** so much in years.

Alice: Very funny, Andrew. I (5) **have been making** all the food, look! Could you please carry it to the living-room?

Andrew: OK. Oh, Alice, (6) **have** you **bought** the soft drinks yet?

Alice: You bought the soft drinks yesterday, remember? You are such an idiot, Andrew.

Andrew: Right, I remember. I think I start to forget things because I (7) **haven't eaten** anything (8) **since** breakfast.

Alice: Don't touch the food, Andrew. I (9) **have been waiting** for this party (10) **for** three weeks now, and I want it to be perfect!

Andrew: You are so boring, little sister!

Das *simple past* und das *past progressive* 4

1 Check-up

Getting ready for a class trip to London

1. While Philip was closing his suitcase, the zipper* broke.
2. While Philip was leaving the house, he lost his mobile phone.
3. While Maria and Sarah were shopping food for the flight, Maria lost her wallet.
4. While Maria and Sarah were driving to the airport, their car broke down.

*__zipper__ – Reißverschluss

2

Philip's notes

1. We boarded the plane at 7 a.m..
2. This was very early.
3. The flight was OK.
4. In London we went to the youth hostel first.
5. At the youth hostel everybody went to their rooms. (Everybody went to their rooms at the youth hostel.)
6. After that we took a sightseeing tour. (We took a sightseeing tour after that.)
7. During the tour Mr. Hunt became sick. (Mr. Hunt became sick during the tour.)
8. In the evening we had supper at an Indian restaurant. (We had supper at an Indian restaurant in the evening.)

3

1. were sleeping
2. was looking
3. was talking
4. were having / was sleeping

4

Thunderstorm in London

1. We were sitting in Hyde Park when it started to rain.
   While we were sitting in Hyde Park, it started to rain.
2. We were visiting the British Museum when it started to rain.
   While we were visiting the British Museum, it started to rain.
3. We were walking through Madame Tussaud's when it started to rain.
   While we were walking through Madame Tussaud's, it started to rain.

4. I was entering Harrod's when it started to rain.
   While I was entering Harrod's, it started to rain.
5. I was looking at elephants when it started to rain.
   While I was looking at elephants, it started to rain.

5

Things happening in London

1. *Andrea:* That's nothing! We **saw** an elephant walk into Harrod's while we **were sitting** across the street in a snack bar.
2. *Sarah:* Oh did you? Well, the police **arrested** me while I **was looking** at CDs in a shop. They thought I wanted to steal them.
3. *Archie:* That's terrible. But I saw something much more terrible. A lady **was lying** in the middle of the street when I **came** around a corner. She was hurt, so I called an ambulance, of course.
4. *Jessica:* At Speaker's Corner a lot of people **were talking** at the same time when I **arrived** and I couldn't understand a word so I decided to leave again. While I **was leaving**, though, suddenly everybody **started** screaming. I turned around and saw a horse running into all the people. It was very frightening. Luckily nobody was hurt.
5. *Alice:* We **were watching** a play at the theatre when suddenly the fire alarm **went** off. It was very strange, and while everybody **was running** to the emergency exits, one of the actors **said**: "Hey, please stay here, the alarm is part of our play." That was very funny.
6. *Khavita:* While we **were eating** lunch at a snack bar, a spider **fell** into my soup. When I finally **stopped** screaming, everybody **was looking** at me.
7. *David:* Aren't big cities crazy? At home in Kansas nothing exciting ever happens. The strangest thing that has happened to me there was that the electricity **went** off while I **was watching** TV.

6

London, 10/7/06

On Tuesday after breakfast we visited a museum that shows a model of the Great Fire of London. In September 1666 a baker forgot to put out the fire in his oven **when** he went to bed. **While** he was sleeping, the fire got out of control and his house started burning. **When** he woke up, he immediately left the house to call for help. **While** people were coming for help, he was already trying to put out the fire, but he could see that it was too late. A strong wind that night made everything worse. **While** the firefighters were trying to save one house, another would start burning because the wind was blowing the fire everywhere. **When** the sun came up the next morning, everybody in London was fighting the flames but the fire went on burning

for five days. **When** the people realized that water was not enough to stop the fire, they destroyed houses and even used gunpowder. Fortunately*, only six people died **while** the fire was burning. That was of course very lucky. After the fire the people started to clean up, and **while** they were doing this, an architect named Christopher Wren was already making plans to rebuild London. This time he used mostly stone, not wood, to build the houses.
I think this was a great museum because the model showed how the fires became bigger and bigger. **While** we were watching it, a lady told us many interesting stories about what happened during the fire.

***fortunately** – glücklicherweise

Test

1

1. John was looking at Big Ben when the bells started to toll.
2. Sarah was looking at Buckingham Palace when suddenly the queen looked out of the window.
3. While Laura and Ben were visiting London Zoo, an ape broke out of its cage.
4. While Mr. Hunt was shopping at a flea market, a thief stole his wallet.
5. Alice and Mary were standing in a queue in front of Madame Tussaud's when they became hungry.

2

Mary writes about Mr. Hunt's terrible class trip to London.
Poor Mr. Hunt, he really had a terrible trip to London. When we **were getting** on the plane, we almost forgot Andy and Lisa because they **were sleeping** in the departure lounge*. Then on the plane there was no food for him. All the pupils **were enjoying** their meals when the stewardess **saw** that they didn't have enough food for everybody. Well, I gave him a bite of my sandwich at least. Later at the youth hostel he became ill. The first three days we were looking at all the sights while poor Mr. Hunt **was lying** in bed. When he was finally healthy again, other terrible things happened: While he **was waiting** in the queue at the British Museum, it **started** to rain and he **got** wet. Then someone **stole** his wallet while he **was shopping** at a flea market. It was a terrible trip for him – but we loved it.

***departure lounge** – Warteraum auf dem Flugplatz

5 Das Passiv

1

Sentences	Active	Passive
Many different sports are played in Britain.	r	(f)
I have been playing Polo for two hours.	(o)	u
In Britain pupils must do sports at school.	(o)	j
American Football is not played in Britain a lot.	p	(t)
Cricket has been played in many countries of the world since about the 19th century.	c	(b)
Sometimes rugby players are hurt.	l	(a)
Polo players wear special clothes.	(l)	t
Have you ever played Polo?	(l)	k

Football was invented in England.

2

Present tense	Simple past	Past participle
drink	drank	**drunk**
burn	**burnt / burned**	**burnt / burned**
sell	**sold**	sold
spend	**spent**	**spent**
play	**played**	**played**
throw	**threw**	thrown
keep	kept	**kept**
eat	**ate**	**eaten**
write	wrote	**written**
pay	**paid**	**paid**
pull	**pulled**	**pulled**
break	**broke**	broken
see	saw	**seen**

3

Sports in Britain

The British are crazy about sports, but many of their games are different from the ones that are played in Europe. Of course they like football. This game was invented in Britain in the last century. Today it is played everywhere. Then there is polo. In this game the ball is hit with sticks by people who sit on horses. Polo has always been played by the rich because they have enough money to buy horses. Rugby is loved in Britain, too. The ball looks like a big egg and is carried, thrown and kicked. The game is stopped for a moment when a player is thrown to the ground. Finally, there's cricket. Many people say that it is a lot like baseball, but it is much more difficult. A game can take a very long time. Sometimes it is even played for many days before there is a winner.

4

1. Today football is played everywhere / all over the world / in many countries.
2. In polo the ball is hit with sticks by people who sit on horses.
3. In rugby the game is stopped for a moment when a player is thrown to the ground.
4. A cricket game can take very long. Sometimes it is even played for days.

5

1. In cricket, the ball isn't thrown from one player to the next.
2. Polo hasn't been played by the poor since it was invented.
3. Rugby isn't hated in Britain.
4. Rugby isn't played with a big banana.
5. Cricket isn't usually played for a month before one team wins.

6

1. When was football invented?
2. Where is football played today?
3. From where is the ball hit in polo?
4. Is the ball kicked in rugby?
5. When is the game stopped for a moment in rugby?
6. For how long is cricket sometimes played?

7

At a football stadium

1. At the entrance tickets are checked.
2. At the entrance everybody is searched for weapons and things that can be thrown.
3. All the exciting scenes are shown again during the game.
4. A lot of songs are sung.
5. A lot of beer and coke is sold.
6. Many sausages are eaten.
7. After the game the stadium is cleaned.

8

Plans for the future

1. All British rugby games will be shown on world wide television.
2. Important rugby games will be organized in every country of the world.
3. An international rugby fan club will be started.
4. It will be called *Rugby Forever*.
5. Rugby balls will be sold all over the world.

9

Then and now

1. Last year rubbish was thrown onto the field, but today it has been taken away and dustbins have been put up.
2. Last year sheep were held in the stables[1], but today horses have been put back.
3. Last year old cars were left next to the field, but today they have been taken to the junk yard[2].
4. Last year the fish and chips kiosk was destroyed, but today a nice restaurant has been built.

1 stable – Stall, **2 junk yard** – Schrottplatz

10

1. by the team captains
2. by helpful parents
3. by a supermarket
4. by the best teams
5. by myself
6. by some older pupils
7. by a teacher and a pupil

Test

1

1. Only in the late twentieth century **has** football been played by women, too.
2. Today even World Championships **are** organized for women.
3. In America football **is** called "soccer".
4. And there it isn't **played** by very many people.
5. Are many games **shown** there on TV? (Are there many games shown on TV?)
6. Sport stars **are** paid a lot of money.

2

1. Bad food is sold to them by the school cafeterias.
2. Computers and televisions are put in their rooms by their parents.
3. At school they aren't taught about good food.
4. In short, they are not shown what a healthy life is like.
5. Then the teachers will be instructed.
6. (In the past) Too many mistakes have been made by the government in the past.
7. Not enough money has been spent on sports.
8. Gymnasiums and sportsfields have not been repaired.
9. A lot of money will be spent to help this young cook.
10. More sports teachers will be hired for the schools.

Präpositionen und *phrasal verbs* 6

1 Check-up

on	~~after~~	under
in	into	~~next to~~
~~until~~	up	down
off	out of	~~on~~
~~under~~	until	during
after	before	~~around~~
into	~~from~~	out of
in front of	~~over~~	behind

2

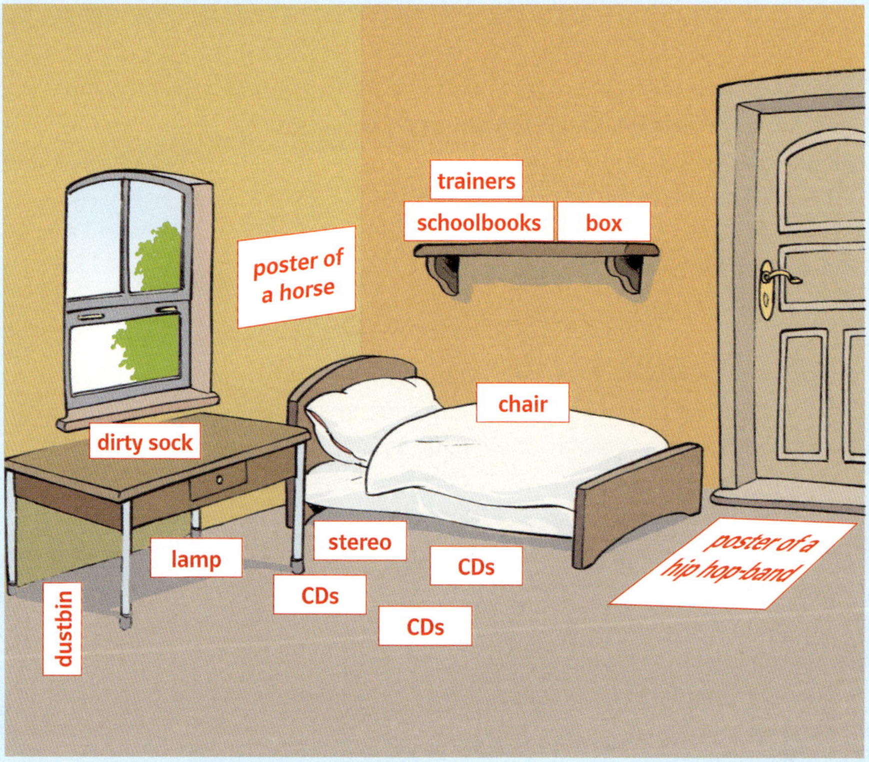

3

1. On 2. During 3. After 4. after 5. in 6. until 7. In 8. at

4

1. out of 2. at 3. at 4. down 5. for 6. to 7. into 8. at 9. out 10. from 11. at 12. to 13. into 14. on 15. in front of 16. around 17. at 18. to 19. at 20. to 21. at 22. until 23. outside

5 Check-up

Sentence	No.
The teacher is putting his books into the bag.	5
She is filling in a worksheet.	6
"Please look after our goldfish while we are away with our tutor group!"	1
He is putting on his trainers for PE.	2
They're looking at a map.	4
They are getting on the bus.	3

6

Phrasal verb	It's time to get up
get up	I get up at 7 o'clock.
turn on (radio)	Then I turn on the radio.
take off (pyjamas)	After that I take off my pyjamas.
get in (shower)	At 7:15 I get in the shower.
turn on / off (water)	I turn the water on. After I'm done, I turn the water off.
put on (clothes)	Then I put on my clothes
look at (myself / mirror)	and look at myself in the mirror.
put into (books)	Before I go downstairs, I put the books into my schoolbag.
	Then I have breakfast in the kitchen.
get on (bike / bus)	After breakfast I get on my bike / the bus and ride to school.
get off	In front of the school I get off my bike / the bus
look for (friends, playground)	and look for my friends in the playground.

7

At the drama club

1. John is looking at himself in the mirror.
2. Andrea is looking up her text in the textbook.
3. Hannah is putting a pistol into a box.
4. Alice is turning the lights on.
5. Philip is putting on his costume.
6. Khavita is taking her wig off.
7. Jill is turning the music up/turning up the music.
8. Mrs. Miller is getting off the stage.

8 9

At the computer club

1. looking for 2. put in 3. look at 4. look them up 5. put it up
6. look at 7. fill it in 8. put it up 9. turn my computer off 10. look after

Test

1

1. Hannah usually gets up **at** 7:30.
2. She meets her friends **at** the bus station.
3. She hates homework because she has to do it **after** school.
4. Hannah's friends usually meet **in** the evenings.
5. They like to meet **in front** of an ice cream place.
6. Then they go **inside** and eat a lot.
7. They leave **after** they have paid and go home.

2

Um die Lösung zu verdeutlichen, ist zusätzlich ein Beispiel zu jeder Präposition angegeben.

Place	Time
on the desk	**on** Monday
under the desk	
in the house	**in** two days
into the bag	
out of the bag	
	after dinner
down the road	
up the street	
to school	
around the house	**around** five o'clock
at my house	**at** six o'clock
over the tree	
	during the school year
	until five o'clock
	before five o'clock

3.1

Hi Anita,

We had a very strange german lesson yesterday. At the beginning of the lesson Mr. Jenkins opened his bag and started to look after **(1)** something. About one minute later he found it – a real bunny. The bunny got onto **(2)** the desk and just sat there. We were all sitting at our desks and looked the bunny up **(3)**. While we were waiting, Mr. Jenkins put a colourful coat on **(4)** and started to talk to **(5)** the bunny in German. That was strange, but then the bunny answered. A bunny that speaks German – wow. Then Mr. Jenkins turned the cassette recorder off **(6)** and the bunny

got off the desk (7) and started to dance. It was a German song and the bunny danced until Mr. Jenkins turned the music on (8) again. After the lesson Mr. Jenkins told us that his parents owned a circus and that they had taught him a lot of tricks. Our homework is terrible, though: we have to take our German dictionaries and have to look at (9) all the words about pets. That's what I must do now.
Bye bye
Hannah

3.2

1. look for something
3. looked at the bunny
6. turned the cassette recorder on
8. turned the music off
9. to look up all the words about pets

Konjunktionen 7

1 Check-up

Sarah was looking forward to Tuesday next week because it was her 13th birthday. Her mother made her a birthday cake and woke her up at six o'clock a.m., because they always do that in her family when it is somebody's birthday. Sarah was very excited although it was so early in the morning. As soon as she got downstairs she ran into the kitchen to look at all the presents she got and spent time opening them until she had to go to school. Of course she forgot to eat breakfast.

2

1. but 2. although 3. because; until 4. as soon as / when 5. because 6. so that 7. until 8. because 9. after 10. until

3

1. so that 2. although / but 3. so that / although 4. when 5. but 6. because / when 7. after / when 8. and 9. as soon as / when

4

Lösungen in Klammern sind theoretisch möglich, aber eher unwahrscheinlich.
Die Hauptvariante ist mit * gekennzeichnet.

1. I hate birthdays **because / (and)** I never know what presents to buy.
2. Philip loves birthdays **because / (and)** he is good at choosing presents.
3. * I never buy presents **because** I never know what to buy.
   I never buy presents **until** it's almost too late.
4. The Millers buy nice presents **although / but** they don't spend much money on them.
5. * Alice is always in a good mood **when / as soon as / after** the party is over.
   Alice is always in a good mood **when / as soon as / after** she is invited to a birthday party.
6. Jill and Brenda are very sad **because** they aren't invited to the birthday party.
7. * I will sing her a love song **when / as soon as / after** the party is over.
   I will sing her a love song **so that** she will kiss me.
8. * Andrew wants to go to the party **because** he is good at choosing presents.
   Andrew wants to go to the party **because / and** he wants to kiss Sarah.
9. Sarah will say "thank you" to her parents **after / when / as soon as** the party is over.

5

1. Until we are sure we really like the person, we shouldn't give presents.
2. As soon as I'm invited to a party, I usually buy a present.
3. When I was thirteen, I never bought birthday presents.
4. Although my parents usually give me a lot of presents for my birthday, I will never buy birthday presents for them.

6

Sarah's mother goes out to buy a present

One week before Sarah's birthday her mother went to the city centre **because** she wanted to find a few birthday presents for her daughter. **When / As soon as** she parked her car, she had a good idea: "Maybe we can buy her a bike **so that** she can get to school faster. That's good **because** then she will have more time for breakfast." **When / As soon as** Sarah's mother went into the shopping mall, she saw a shop for motorcycles and thought: "We won't buy her a motorcycle **until** she is 18." Then she saw a shop for make-up. She went inside and thought. "She loves lipsticks **because / and** she wants to look nice at parties." Then she went on and found a bicycle-shop. **When / As soon as** she saw a shop assistant, she asked him for a bike for her daughter **and** he showed her one that she liked. **Although** it was very expensive, she bought it **and** went home – she was very excited.

7

Sarah's father went shopping, too

1. Sarah's father went shopping that day, too, **but / although** he went to a different part of town.
2. He works a lot **so that / and** he and his wife didn't have much time to plan the birthday shopping.
3. He thought: "We have to buy Sarah a new bike **because** her bike is much too small for her now.
4. She will like that **because** then she will be able to sleep longer in the mornings.
5. **When / As soon as** he saw a make-up shop, he thought:
6. "I will not buy a new lipstick for her **because** she already has got about thirty in her bathroom."
7. Then Sarah's father was very hungry **so that / and** he went to the food court and ordered a pizza.
8. **When / As soon as** he left the shopping centre a few minutes later, he had a good idea.
9. I will buy a new German computer programme for her **so that** she can get better marks at school.

Test

1 10

1. because 2. but / and 3. after / when 4. until 5. so that / until 6. because 7. because / although 8. although 9. so that 10. when 11. after / when

2

1. Although he kissed me this year, I will invite Andrew.
2. Until my parents have talked to each other about my presents, I will not let them go shopping next year.
3. Not possible
4. When they arrive, I will give a little present to every guest.
5. Not possible

3

Die Hauptvariante ist mit * gekennzeichnet.

- * Birthdays are great **because** you get a lot of presents.
  Birthdays are great **although / but** they cost a lot of money.
- * Buying presents is fun **although / but** they cost a lot of money.
- * Parties are great for the parents, too, **although / but** they must do all the work.
- * Parties are great for the parents, too, **although** they cost a lot of money.

- * Sarah helped her parents clean up the house **after / when / as soon as** her friends left.
  (Sarah helped her parents clean up the house **because / when** she got another bad mark in a German test.) Dieser Satz ist möglich, ergibt aber im Zusammenhang der Geschichte keinen Sinn.
- * Sarah didn't use her new German programme **until / although** she got another bad mark in a German test.
- * The next day Sarah used her new lipstick **and** rode her bike to school.
- * The next day at school Andrew didn't kiss her **but** he smiled at her.
- * Sarah was very happy **when / because / although** Andrew kissed her again a week later.
- * Sarah was very happy **although / when / because / after / as soon as** her friends left.

8 Tipps zum Lernen von Vokabeln

1 Check-up

s	f	y	z	u	d	l	c	f	a	d	b	**m**
e	**t**	**e**	**l**	**e**	**v**	**i**	**s**	**i**	**o**	**n**	j	**i**
y	d	e	z	u	h	g	p	l	e	p	o	**r**
e	f	t	w	s	t	j	x	w	l	**p**	e	**r**
l	**i**	**v**	**i**	**n**	**g**	**r**	**o**	**o**	**m**	**i**	d	**o**
a	f	e	z	**l**	**a**	**m**	**p**	r	r	**l**	g	**r**
a	**c**	v	n	d	s	e	s	d	r	**l**	z	t
s	**u**	h	i	q	j	m	d	j	g	**o**	f	a
e	**p**	u	**k**	**i**	**t**	**c**	**h**	**e**	**n**	**w**	o	i
c	**b**	u	s	i	l	o	a	w	r	u	k	**s**
o	**o**	u	y	t	t	w	z	j	i	d	h	**t**
e	**a**	e	**s**	d	j	**c**	**u**	**p**	d	k	r	**a**
a	**r**	j	**o**	l	p	c	u	j	i	p	r	**i**
p	**d**	g	**f**	d	w	i	o	e	d	j	u	**r**
c	h	u	**a**	e	a	j	u	o	n	e	h	**s**

2

Helen's house

Küche:

1. sink
2. refrigerator
3. glass
4. cup
5. plate
6. microwave
7. freezer

Bad:

9. shower
9. toilet
10. towel
11. toothpaste
12. toothbrush
13. soap

Wohnzimmer:

14. couch
15. stereo
16. phone
17. armchair
18. coffee table

Schlafzimmer:

19. bed
20. pillow
21. pyjamas

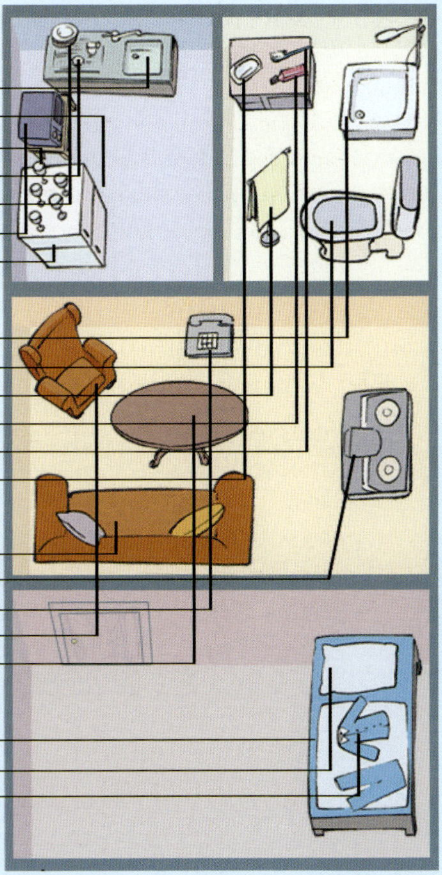

3

What Helen does in her house

1. She **does** the dishes in the sink.
2. She **switches** the stereo **on** when she wants to listen to music.
3. She **sets** the coffee table when her friends come to visit her.
4. She **answers** the phone when it rings.
5. She **relaxes** on the couch after school.
6. She **has** breakfast every morning.
7. She **takes** a shower every morning before she goes to school.
8. She **brushes** her teeth three times a day with her toothbrush.
9. She **switches** all the lights **off** in the house before she **goes** to bed.

4

In the kitchen

In the cupboard	In the refrigerator	Machines that help you
plate	sausage	stove
glass	cheese	dishwasher
knife	milk	refrigerator
fork	juice	microwave oven
spoon	lemonade	coffeemaker
	butter	freezer
		blender

5

1. b 2. c 3. a, b 4. c 5. a 6. a, c 7. c 8. b, c

6

1. Helen and her friend 11

3	"Sure. Hang on a minute."
8	"Bye Susan."
7	"OK, then I'll go by myself. Bye Helen."
4	"Hi, Susan. What's up?"
6	"No, I'm too tired. I was up late last night. There was a great party at Edward's house."
2	"Hi Dan, this is Susan. Can I speak to Helen, please?"
1	"Hello, Luton 3461394, Dan Mitchel speaking."
5	"Not much. I just wanted to ask you if we're going running this afternoon."

2. Helen and the doctor's office 12

4	"Yes, could you please ask her to call me back."
2	"Good afternoon. This is Helen Mitchel speaking. May I speak to Dr. Miller, please?"
7	"Good bye."
1	"Dr. Miller's practice, Nurse Dana speaking. How may I help you?"
3	"Hold on a minute … I'm sorry, but Dr.Miller is very busy at the moment. May I take a message?"
6	"Thank you very much. Good bye."
5	"Certainly, Mrs. Mitchel. Dr. Miller will ring you as soon as possible."

7

Informal (to a friend)	**Formal (to a stranger)**
hi	good afternoon
What's up?	How may I help you?
OK	
bye	good bye
Can I speak to …	May I speak to …
Hang on a minute	Could you hold on a minute please?
	Could you please ask her …
	May I take a message?

8

1. What answering machines tell you 13

1. Hi, this is Andrews machine. Leave a **message** after the beep.
2. Hello, you've reached the Millers. Sorry we're not **home** right now, but if you leave a message, we will **call** you back as soon as possible.
3. Hello. This is Mrs. Anderson's office. We can't **answer** the phone right now, but please leave your name and **number** and we will call you back **as soon as** possible.
4. Hello. You've **reached** "Shoes and More" in Bond Street. We are **closed** in the mornings. Our opening hours are **from** 1 p.m. **to** 8 p.m. daily. We look forward to your **visit**.

2. What you say to answering machines 14

1. Hi, Alice, **this** is Helen. Something really exciting happened at school today. **Call** me back soon!

2. Good afternoon, this is Mr. Briand. I have got a **question** about my son's class test. **Could** you please call me back. My **number** is 020-01324984. Thank you very much.
3. Hey Andy, **let's** go to the park today to play some football. I'll be there in 20 **minutes**. Don't **worry** about the English homework, Mr. Miller is **ill**.
4. Good morning. I would **like** to order two tickets for "Dracula's Return" tonight **at** 6 p.m. My number is 020-20457653. **Thank** you, good bye.

3. What people say when they call back

15

1. Hey Helen, you sound so excited. I was out running when you called, so sorry. But when I came back home, the phone rang and this boy from form 10 called and wanted to know what I would be doing on Saturday evening. I'm so excited. What happened to you? Did Matthew ask you out? That would be great. Maybe we could all go out together to see a movie on Saturday. Call back soon!!!!!!

16

2. Good evening Mr. Briand. I'm returning your call from this afternoon. I'm afraid I can't talk to you about your son on the phone. This is a very serious case which I would like to discuss in person. I believe your son will need extra help in more than one subject. Please visit me during my office hours: Tuesdays from ten to eleven o'clock.

17

3. Wow, that's great news. Are you sure? Miller has never been ill before. How long will he be gone? A year?? Hahahahaha! I'll see you in the park. Maybe we'll go to the shops later and buy the new ego-shooter. My mom will kill me, but I don't care. Andy.

18

4. Good afternoon. This is "City Center Films". We are returning your call from this morning. I'm sorry to tell you that "Dracula's Return" is sold out for tonight. We'll be showing it again tomorrow and the day after tomorrow at 8 p.m. Good bye.

1. Alice
c) has been asked out by a boy from form 10.
e) hopes that Helen has been asked out by Matthew.

2. The teacher
d) wants to organize some extra help for Mr. Briand's son.
e) invites Mr. Briand to his office on Tuesday.

3. Andy
a) is very surprised that Mr. Miller is ill.
d) wants to go to the shops later.

4. Tickets for "Dracula's Return"
a) have all been sold.
d) can be bought for tomorrow's performance at 8 p.m.

9

s	h	o	p	s	l	e	r	g	a	h	g	u	j	s	o	r	l
u	d	z	s	h	o	n	i	t	r	y	o	n	c	t	u	l	l
p	a	h	z	o	o	e	j	i	p	s	w	l	o	t	a	e	r
e	c	g	t	p	k	i	z	r	o	w	t	e	w	m	e	i	t
r	o	z	r	a	f	e	d	n	b	o	o	k	s	t	o	r	e
m	y	r	e	s	o	j	u	c	i	e	h	u	o	r	x	g	j
a	o	l	e	s	r	q	t	o	f	c	z	b	j	e	v	j	o
r	s	h	i	i	k	l	o	s	b	f	e	s	a	g	u	i	o
k	o	u	t	s	v	h	u	t	l	a	r	z	t	k	r	e	w
e	j	g	c	t	e	u	i	o	u	y	c	f	r	z	e	i	r
t	m	h	z	a	m	t	r	t	w	z	t	r	e	w	h	r	j
g	g	h	j	n	u	i	i	o	z	r	e	w	r	z	u	o	y
d	i	k	t	t	p	f	s	f	f	h	j	k	l	d	j	i	o
e	a	f	t	z	u	d	g	l	o	o	k	a	r	o	u	n	d
p	i	m	t	l	r	w	s	f	h	z	e	s	x	g	j	i	s
a	x	g	h	s	u	i	o	c	u	t	r	e	i	l	d	r	e
r	c	h	t	z	h	i	o	h	o	h	u	r	x	d	f	u	l
t	t	i	z	r	l	o	t	u	t	o	l	p	s	r	e	w	l
m	v	g	h	z	h	l	p	t	h	e	l	p	x	d	h	z	u
e	n	k	i	s	h	o	e	s	t	o	r	e	m	u	t	e	d
n	r	t	k	s	g	l	o	h	j	b	u	y	n	r	z	e	a
t	g	e	i	t	e	i	m	n	v	s	g	t	r	j	r	r	z
s	a	s	k	k	z	r	s	u	o	z	l	l	v	r	l	s	t
t	l	i	z	r	n	i	c	e	f	v	y	c	h	e	a	p	d
o	v	h	z	u	i	s	w	c	b	h	n	u	i	a	r	c	f
r	j	t	e	s	e	t	u	l	s	e	v	n	n	t	g	r	t
e	x	p	e	n	s	i	v	e	s	f	t	w	k	u	e	k	o

Nouns	Adjectives	Verbs
book store	beautiful	try on
department store	expensive	look for
shop assistant	cheap	look around
gift shop	cool	buy
shoe store	nice	sell
supermarket	ugly	cost
bakery	large	ask
shop	small	help

10

At the **shoe shop**

Shop assistant: Good morning, may I help you?

You: Yes please. **I'm looking for** some new shoes.

Shop assistant: Alright, let's see. Yes, I've got some very **cool / nice / beautiful** ones over here. How do you like them?

You: Not so much. How about those over there, they look really **cool / nice / beautiful**.

Shop assistant: Would you like to **try** them **on**? What's your size?

You: My shoe size is 5 ½, but could you first tell me how much they **cost**, please?

Shop assistant: They are 80 pounds.

You: Wow, that's too **expensive** for me. Have you got some cheaper ones, too?

Shop assistant: I'm sorry, these are the cheapest shoes we have.

You: Well, I think I will have to look somewhere else then. Good bye.

Shop assistant: Good bye.

11

Supermarket	Bakery	Book store	Gift shop
bread	bread	postcard	pen
cake	cake	book	postcard
vegetables		map	lipstick
milk		magazine	poster
butter			teddy bear
fruit			CD
fish			
crisps			
chocolate			

12

Situation	Nr.
Du lehnst die Hilfe eines Verkäufers ab und sagst ihm, dass du dich nur ein wenig umschauen möchtest.	3
Du verabschiedest dich freundlich aus dem Geschäft.	9
Du fragst die Verkäuferin, ob sie dasselbe Produkt noch eine Nummer kleiner hat.	5
Du bringst deine Begeisterung über eine Farbe zum Ausdruck.	8
Du fragst höflich um Hilfe.	1
Du fragst höflich, ob du ein bestimmtes T-shirt anprobieren darfst.	4
Du bedankst dich und sagst, dass du es dir noch einmal überlegen möchtest.	10
Du fragst den Verkäufer, ob er nicht etwas Ähnliches billiger anzubieten hat.	7
Du fragst, wo du die Milch finden kannst.	6
Du bittest die Verkäuferin, dir beim Suchen nach einem Geschenk für einen Freund zu helfen.	2

Test

1

1. In the morning Helen's **alarm clock** goes off and she gets up and takes a shower.
2. Helen uses **soap** to wash her hands.
3. Before breakfast she takes the plates from the **cupboard** and puts them on the table.
4. After that she puts **water** into the coffee maker and sits down.
5. When Helen leaves the house, she switches all the lights **off**.
6. Her answering machine says: "Hello, this is Helen Mitchel's machine. Sorry I'm not home right now but if you leave a **message / number**, I'll call you back."
7. This afternoon she went shopping. In the first three shops she just looked **around** but in the last shop she bought a book.
8. When she came home, her friend called on the phone and said: "**Hi Helen**, what's up?"
9. Later that evening she went to the living room, sat down in the **armchair** and watched TV.

2

look for
living room
dish washer
hold on
supermarket
look around
cupboard
microwave oven
call back
gift shop
answering machine
shop assistant
hang on
department store
try on

9 Leseverstehen: Einen geschriebenen Text verstehen

1 Check-up

1. Sarah's friend is unhappy at school.
2. Sarah wrote this letter to a youth magazine.
3. If someone is "skinny" it means that he / she is thin.
4. Sarah wrote this letter in April.

2

1. This text is about a big problem that can be found at many schools.
2. A bully is someone who usually has got a problem.
   A bully is someone who is not nice to other people.
3. The text says that last year many pupils had problems with bullies.
4. The text wants to help people who are bullied.

3

Informationen, die du zur Beantwortung der Fragen brauchst, sind in der Lösung blau. Wörter, die dir vermutlich noch nicht bekannt sind, sind unterstrichen.

Bullying at schools: an everyday problem!

More and more pupils feel bullied at school. Bullies **call other pupils names**, they **tell lies** about their victims, **steal** from them, or even **attack** them. Last year **two-thirds of all pupils in the U.K. said that they had been bullied** in some form during the school year.

Why do bullies bully?

Psychologists say that **most bullies have problems themselves**. They **feel unsure** about themselves because they might **have trouble at home or at school**. They may also **feel alone** and **think they will find friends** by making fun of other people. Often they even want to be like the person they bully. **They are jealous** and therefore they attack.

Who are the victims?

The people who are bullied, the victims, are often people who **show that they are weak** because it's much easier to attack a weak person than a strong one. Often the **victims look different** from other people **(slim, overweight, strange clothes)**, or they are **not good at certain things** (often **sports**), or they may **not have many friends**. Any kind of weakness attracts bullies.

Help

If you need help because someone bullies you, call **the Bully-Line: 944-3454**.

4

Word	Meaning
to call s.o. names	Du kennst die einzelnen Wörter. Da du weißt, dass ein Mobber *(bully)* nicht nett ist, kannst du erschließen, dass die Namen, die er sich einfallen lässt, sicher keine Kosenamen sind: **jemanden beschimpfen**
victim	Wird im letzten Abschnitt erklärt: **Opfer**
psychologist	Kannst du vom Deutschen ableiten: **Psychologe**
unsure	Du kennst *sure* (sicher). Die Vorsilbe *-un* verkehrt den Sinn eines Wortes normalerweise in das Gegenteil: **unsicher**
overweight	Du kennst *over* = über und *weight* = Gewicht: **übergewichtig** oder **dick**
weakness	Du kennst *weak* = schwach. Die Nachsilbe *-ness* macht aus einem Adjektiv ein Nomen: **Schwäche**

5

Bully

What?
- call pupils names
- tell lies about others
- steal
- attack

Why?
- have problems at school or at home
- feel unsure
- feel alone
- want friends
- are jealous

Victims?
- look different (overweight, slim, strange clothes)
- not good at things (sports)
- don't have friends
- show weakness

6

	right	wrong	nit
This text is about how to react to a bully.	x		
There is not much you can do against a bully.		x	
It's OK to call the police if a bully bothers you.			x
Friends can help you against a bully.	x		
Bullies often are alone themselves.			x
It doesn't help to hit a bully.	x		

7

Informationen, die du zur Beantwortung der Fragen brauchst, sind in der Lösung blau. Wörter, die dir vermutlich noch nicht bekannt sind, sind unterstrichen.

What can you do against bullies?

There are **many things you can do** if someone tries to bully you. Maybe you will have to try different methods until you succeed.

The first approach is **to ignore the bully**. If he calls you names, don't react! **Bullies often get bored** if their victim does not seem to be hurt by their attacks. The next step must be to get your **friends to help** you. They can **help you by just being with you** while you are at school, for example. **Bullies like to bother pupils who are alone, because it's easier**. Your **friends can also defend you** against the bully. If a bully sees that your friends help you and don't leave you alone, he will usually back off. If you can't ignore the bully because you are really hurt or you don't have enough friends to help you, **talk to adults** about it. That could be your **parents, or a teacher, or anyone else you think might be able to help you.**

Never hit a bully. That usually **makes things worse** and **might get you into trouble yourself**. However, **never run away** from them **or show them that they hurt your feelings**. If you do that, you can be sure that the bully will go on bothering you.

Always remember: **it's the bully who is wrong**, not you! You have the right to be the way you want to be. If the bully doesn't like that, it's his problem, not yours. If you want to win against a bully **you must be strong**!

8

1. If someone bullies you, you should first ignore the bully and then ask your friends for help. If that doesn't help, **catch the bully on his way home and give him a good beating**.
2. Bullies like to bully people who are alone. That's why you should try not to be alone when "your" bully is around. Always ask a friend to come with you. If you

don't have friends, just **run away when you see the bully, that way he can't bother you**.

3. **It is your fault if a bully picks on you. So if the bully says that your clothes are stupid, buy new clothes and the problem will be solved.** If that doesn't work, talk to adults who might be able to help you.

9

Word	**Meaning**	**Not so important, means something like**
method	Kannst du vom Deutschen ableiten → **Methode**	
to succeed		Wenn du die verschiedenen Methoden verstanden hast, muss *to succeed* so etwas heißen wie „es schaffen" (tatsächlich heißt es **erfolgreich sein**).
approach		Da nun eine Aufzählung folgt *(the first, the next)*, bedeutet *approach* wohl so etwas wie „Art und Weise" (tatsächlich heißt es **Vorgehensweise**).
to ignore	Kannst du aus dem Deutschen ableiten: **ignorieren**	
to bother	Kannst du aus dem Zusammenhang erschließen: es ist das, was Mobber tun: **jdn. ärgern**	
to back off	*back* heißt „zurück": **sich zurückziehen**	

10

Dos and Don'ts when you are bullied

Dos (what you should do)	**Don'ts (what you shouldn't do)**
- ignore the bully - ask friends to help you - they can be with you or defend you - talk to adults (parents, teacher, others that can help)	- hit a bully - don't run away - don't show that your feelings are hurt

I must always be **strong**.

11

Suzie was bullied by **a girl**.
She **ignored the bully**.
Now she **has a lot of new friends**.

12

Informationen, die du zur Beantwortung der Fragen brauchst, sind in der Lösung blau. Wörter, die dir vermutlich noch nicht bekannt sind, sind unterstrichen.

Suzie's experience with a bully

There was a bully (who I barely even knew, so she had no reason to start being mean to me) who just recently started giving me trouble. I mean, she just **called me names and tried to embarrass me in front of the whole class. I just totally ignored her,** remained strong, and when she tried to bully me right in front of **boys she likes, they saw that she was stupid and I was nice!** Suddenly **her friends started to like me** and feel sorry for me and didn't like her any more. **THAT made her so incredibly angry and jealous!** And that, my friends, was sweet victory. **She soon gave up and I had a lot of new friends**.

The best thing to remember here, people, is that your **bully feeds on how bad he/she makes you feel.** This is a sign that that person is insecure and immature! **Be strong out there, and you'll win more friends**. This is something that will give you a happier, easier life, now and in the future.

Suzie

13

One day a **girl** started bullying Suzie. That was very strange because Suzie didn't **know** her very well. But Suzie just **ignored** the bully and remained **strong**. Suzie really won the conflict when the bully tried to bother Suzie **in front of** her friends. The bully's friends didn't react like she had hoped they would. They saw that the bully was **stupid** and Suzie was **nice**. So the bully lost her **friends** and Suzie had **a lot of** new friends. Suzie believes that the most important thing to know about bullies is that they like it when they see that their victim feels **bad / hurt**. That's why it is important to stay **strong** .

14

Word	**Meaning**	**Not so important, means something like**
barely		Muss so etwas wie „nicht gut" bedeuten, denn so wird es im *summary* wiedergegeben: *barely* heißt **kaum**.
to embarrass		Eine weitere Art und Weise, wie Mobber ihre Opfer angreifen. Da es vor Freunden geschieht, muss es so etwas heißen wie **bloßstellen**.
to remain		*I* und *strong* genügen, um zu verstehen, was sie sagt. *To remain* heißt **bleiben**.
to feed	Das musst du wahrscheinlich nachschlagen. Es heißt „sich ernähren", aber im Bezug auf Tiere, nicht auf Menschen. Hier könnte man es z. B. mit **leben von** übersetzen.	

15

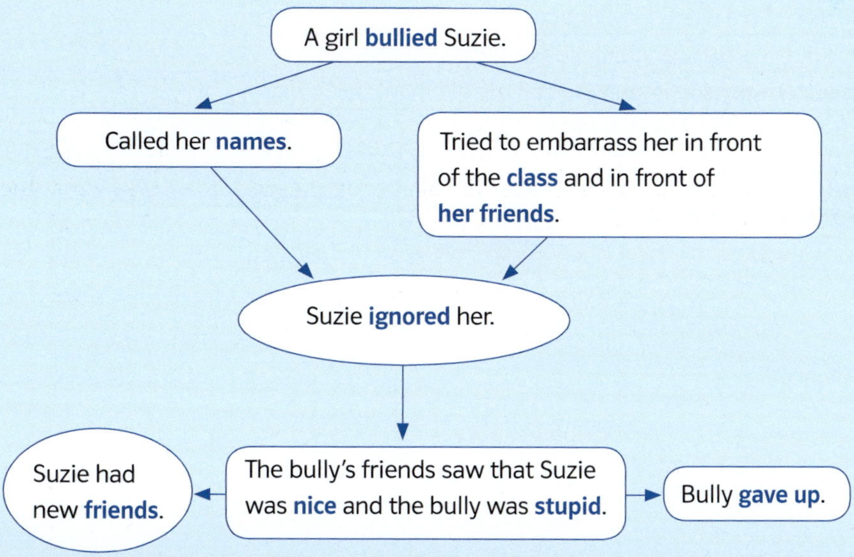

10 Hörverstehen: Einen gesprochenen Text verstehen

1 Check-up 19

1. c) an alarm clock is going off
2. b) a police car is driving by
3. a) a woman is crying for help
4. a) two cars are crashing into each other

2 20

1. a) Inspector Atkinson's radio alarm wakes her up in the morning.
2. c) The people are angry because the underground is late.
3. b) Mrs. Atkinson is buying a newspaper.
4. b) Mrs. Atkinson is having breakfast in the police cafeteria.

3 21

	r	w	nit
Inspector Atkinson is having a great morning.		x	
She dreamed about a great birthday party last night.		x	
Mr. Mitchum dreamed about a murder last night.			x
Something terrible happened in Bold Street last night.	x		
Mr. MacAllister was a millionaire.		x	
An old man saw everything and called the police.	x		
Inspector Atkinson is going to call the old man right away.	x		

4 22

Killer Joe and Revolver Andy

5 23

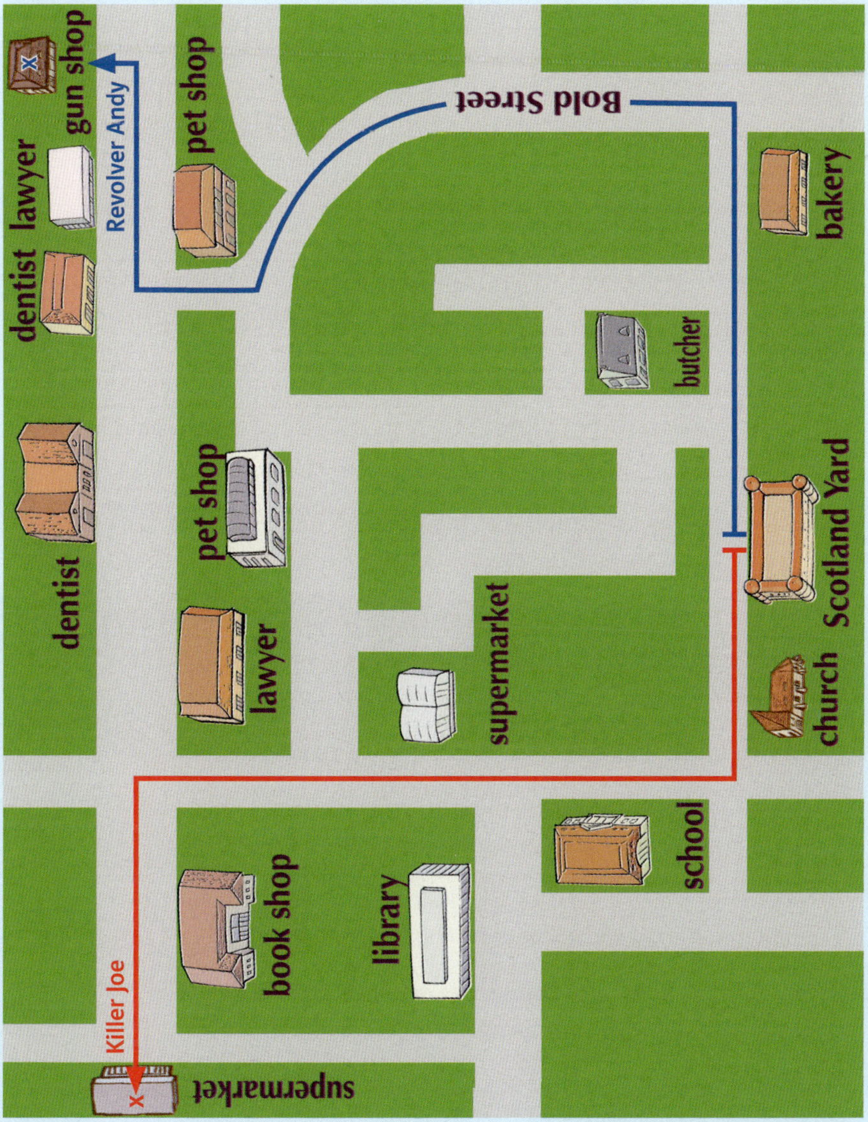
gun shop
lawyer
dentist
dentist
Revolver Andy
pet shop
Bold Street
pet shop
lawyer
supermarket
butcher
bakery
Scotland Yard
church
school
book shop
library
Killer Joe
supermarket

6 24–25

Question	Suspect No. 1	Suspect No. 2
What have you been doing since you left prison?	**looking for work; no success**	**working in brother's gun shop**
What were you doing last night at 2 o'clock in the morning?	**running in Bold Street**	**sleeping**
Do you know where Bold Street is?	**yes, runs there**	**no**
If "yes": Did you see or hear anything strange there last night?	**yes, saw someone shoot a man**	**no, wasn't there**
Do you own a gun?	**no**	**yes, says he'll get it**
Do you know Andrew MacAllister?	**no**	**yes, he likes his girlfriend**

7

1. The name "Revolver Andy" shows that he is a bad man. ☐
2. Two people say they saw a man who looked like Revolver Andy in Bold Street last night, but Revolver Andy says he wasn't there. ☒
3. People who wear dark coats and hats are always suspicious*. ☐
4. Revolver Andy could easily hide the gun under his coat, but Killer Joe couldn't. He was wearing shorts and a T-shirt. ☒
5. Revolver Andy works in a gun-shop. It was easy for him to take a gun from the shop and kill Andrew MacAllister. ☒
6. Revolver Andy has no witnesses to back up his story that he was sleeping last night. Killer Joe was seen by Mr. Maple. ☐
7. Revolver Andy knows Andrew MacAllister and doesn't like him, because MacAllister likes Andy's girlfriend. ☒
8. Revolver Andy talks about MacAllister in the simple past tense, although Inspector Atkinson hasn't told him that he was killed. ☒
9. Revolver Andy is not friendly to Mrs. Atkinson. Killer Joe is much nicer. ☐

*__suspicious__ – verdächtig

Hörtexte

2 20

A morning in inspector Atkinson's life

1.

"Good morning, it's 6:15 a.m., ladies and gentlemen. Once again, here's the Morning Show with Dave Sinclair and the best music in London …"

2.

"Ladies and Gentlemen, we are sorry to announce that the train to Piccadilly Circus will be fifteen minutes late due to a defect in the lighting system."

„Again"
„Just like every morning"
"I want my money back"
"This flippin' underground"
"I'll be late for work again"

3.

Newsagent: Good morning, Inspector Atkinson. How are you today?
Atkinson: All right, thank you. How about yourself? *The Times* please, as always.
Newsagent: Here you are, any other newspaper for you today, Madam?
Atkinson: No, thanks, just *The Times*. Nothing really happened yesterday, did it?
Newsagent: Well, there was a murder in Bold Street …"

4.

Policeman: Hey Atkinson, how's the coffee this morning?
Atkinson: Terrible, as always. Do you know anything about the murder last night in Bold Street?
Policeman: Naw, nothing – only that you're in charge.
Atkinson: Great!
Policeman: Well, enjoy your breakfast, and have a nice day.
Atkinson: Thanks.

3 21

Mrs. Atkinson meets her colleague, Mr. Mitchum, in her office.

Mr. Mitchum: Good morning, how are you today?
Inspector Atkinson: Could be better. I didn't sleep too well last night. I had a terrible dream.
Mr. Mitchum: That's awful. What did you dream about?
Inspector Atkinson: It was about a murder in Bond Street, and I just couldn't find out who it was.

Mr. Mitchum:	Well, maybe it wasn't really a dream. Somebody was murdered last night at two o'clock a.m., but not in Bond Street. It was in Bold Street.
Inspector Atkinson:	Yes, I already heard.
Mr. Mitchum:	Oh, did you? That's good, because the boss said he wants you to find the murderer.
Inspector Atkinson:	Great, and I thought I could have a quiet day at the office. What do we already know about the case?
Mr. Mitchum:	Well, the victim was shot from behind with a gun. It happened in the middle of the street. His name was Andrew MacAllister. The murderer didn't take any money from him.
Inspector Atkinson:	What do we know about Mr. MacAllister?
Mr. Mitchum:	He was 34 years old and lived in a small flat in South London. He worked as a bus driver and wasn't married. He wasn't rich but he had a lot of friends. Quite a normal person, I would say.
Inspector Atkinson:	Any witnesses?
Mr. Mitchum:	Well, there is an old man who couldn't sleep. He was sitting next to his window when he heard the shot. When he looked out of the window, he saw two people in the street. He said we could call him and he could describe them to us.
Inspector Atkinson:	Not a bad start. Let's do it. What's his name?
Mr. Mitchum:	It's Mr. Maple.

4 22

Inspector Atkinson is talking to a witness, Mr. Maple.

Mr. Maple:	Hello, London 020-76546754. Mr. Maple speaking.
Inspector Atkinson:	Good morning Mr. Maple. This is Inspector Atkinson, Scotland Yard …
Mr. Maple:	Oh, yes, I called the police this morning because this terrible thing happened, and I couldn't sleep all night because my foot hurt so much, you know my grandson stepped on it two weeks ago and I can't walk anymore, you know my grandson's name is Mark and he is such a nice boy …
Inspector Atkinson:	Oh really, Mr. Maple, that's nice to hear, but I really didn't call to hear about your grandson. You said you saw two people in the street last night, after you heard the shot …
Mr. Maple:	Yes, that's right. It was terrible, there was this shot and I looked out of the window and … you know it's just like in that book I read two months ago where a goldfish is murdered …

Inspector Atkinson: Yes, I agree, Mr. Maple, a wonderful book. What did these people look like?
Mr. Maple: You know, it was quite dark, I couldn't see much.
Inspector Atkinson: Let me help you: were they tall, short, slim, fat?
Mr. Maple: Hm, one was tall – very tall indeed, the other was quite normal, I would say.
Inspector Atkinson: OK. How about their weight?
Mr. Maple: The tall one was very slim, and the normal one was … hmmmmmm … normal, I would say.
Inspector Atkinson: Hmm, now, did you see their clothes?
Mr. Maple: One was wearing a long dark coat – that was the tall one, I think.
Inspector Atkinson: And the other one?
Mr. Maple: I'm not sure, I think he just wore a t-shirt and shorts, isn't that strange?
Inspector Atkinson: It is indeed. Well, hmm, could you see their hair?
Mr. Maple: I think the normal one had very long hair – almost like a lady – these people today, they look so strange. When I was young, women had long hair and men …
Inspector Atkinson: What about the tall man's hair?
Mr. Maple: I don't know.
Inspector Atkinson: What do you mean. You don't know.
Mr. Maple: Well, like any good man, he wore a hat.
Inspector Atkinson: Right, I should have known. Is there anything else you think might be important for me to know?
Mr. Maple: I'm not sure but in that book I read, you know, the one about the goldfish …
Inspector Atkinson: Thank you for your help Mr. Maple. Good bye.
Mr. Maple: Good bye.

5 **23**

Inspector Atkinson is going to visit the two people Mr. Maple saw last night. Mr. Mitchum tells inspector Atkinson where they live.

Inspector Atkinson: Here we are, the two people that Mr. Maple saw are Revolver Andy and Killer Joe. Do you know where they live?
Mr. Mitchum: Yes, I do but I don't remember their addresses. I only remember how to get there.
Inspector Atkinson: OK. Tell me! Where does Killer Joe live?

Mr. Mitchum:	That's easy. When you leave our building, turn left and follow the street all the way to the church. There you turn right and follow that street to the second street. There you … hmm … yes, … no … hmm yes, you turn left and go down the street until you're in front of the supermarket. His flat is in the same house.
Inspector Atkinson:	Yeah, that's easy enough: left, right, left, to the supermarket. How about Revolver Andy?
Mr. Mitchum:	That's a little more difficult, let me think … OK: turn right when you leave the house, follow the street to the bakery and then turn left. Have you got that?
Inspector Atkinson:	Yes: right and then left to the bakery.
Mr. Mitchum:	No, not to the bakery but at the bakery!
Inspector Atkinson:	Right … OK, what next?
Mr. Mitchum:	Follow that street to the end. There you can either turn left or right. You want to turn right here. Not left, right. Got that?
Inspector Atkinson:	I'm not stupid, am I?
Mr. Mitchum:	Alright. Now: you walk down this street. You will walk past a pet shop, a dentist's, and a lawyer's, before you reach a gun shop on the left side of the street. Revolver Andy lives under the gun shop – I think the shop is his brother's.
Inspector Atkinson:	Thanks, sounds like a very nice place to visit a suspect. See you later.

6

Inspector Atkinson goes to pay a visit to the two suspects. First she talks to Killer Joe, then to Revolver Andy.

1. Killer Joe. In the flat above the supermarket 24

Doorbell rings.

Joe:	Who's there?
Inspector Atkinson:	Inspector Atkinson, Scotland Yard. Please open the door!
Joe:	Why? I haven't done anything.
Inspector Atkinson:	That's what I'm here to find out. Open the door!
Joe:	Alright …, come in.
Inspector Atkinson:	Thank you, very kind of you. Well Joe, I've got a few questions for you.
Joe:	Go ahead!
Inspector Atkinson:	What have you been doing since you left prison two weeks ago?

Joe: I've been looking for a job, of course. I'm a good boy now.
Inspector Atkinson: Of course. Did you find one?
Joe: Nope, not yet. It's not easy if you come straight from prison.
Inspector Atkinson: That's true. Now, what were you doing last night at two o'clock in the morning?
Joe: I was out running, why?
Inspector Atkinson: Running? At two o'clock in the morning?
Joe: Is that against the law?
Inspector Atkinson: No, not at all, but it's strange, isn't it?
Joe: Not for me, I couldn't sleep, so I went running. I often do that.
Inspector Atkinson: OK. Do you know where Bold Street is?
Joe: Let me think … of course … it's where I always run. It's a nice and quiet street. Not much traffic. A good street to go running.
Inspector Atkinson: Did you see or hear anything strange there last night?
Joe: Yes, I saw somebody shoot a man there at two o'clock when I was there.
Inspector Atkinson: You saw what …?
Joe: I saw somebody shoot a man there at two o'clock when I was there.
Inspector Atkinson: Why didn't you tell me earlier?
Joe: You didn't ask.
Inspector Atkinson: Why didn't you call the police?
Joe: Because I was too busy running away and I was afraid they would say I shot the man.
Inspector Atkinson: What did the murderer look like?
Joe: He was wearing a long dark coat and a hat. He was tall and slim.
Inspector Atkinson: A dark coat and a hat, aha … Do you own a gun?
Joe: No, I don't, I told you, I'm a good boy now.
Inspector Atkinson: Do you know Andrew MacAllister?
Joe: Andrew Mac what?
Inspector Atkinson: Allister … Andrew MacAllister. He's the man who was murdered.
Joe: No, never heard of him. Was that it? I have to go out and look for a job. Oh, by the way: could I work for Scotland Yard? I'm sure I would be a great detective …
Inspector Atkinson: Good bye Joe, and good luck.

2. Revolver Andy. Under the gun shop 25

Inspector Atkinson (to himself): That's a strange doorbell.

Andy:	Who's there?
Inspector Atkinson:	Inspector Atkinson, Scotland Yard. Please open the door!
Andy:	Leave me alone, or I'll go and get my gun.
Inspector Atkinson:	Relax! I've just got a few questions. We need your help.
Andy:	Forget it. I'm not talking to the police any more.
Inspector Atkinson:	If you don't open I will send the police to arrest you.
Andy:	Alright, what do you want?
Inspector Atkinson:	Thank you. I would like to ask you a few questions.
Andy:	Well …?
Inspector Atkinson:	What have you been doing since you left prison two weeks ago?
Andy:	Working.
Inspector Atkinson:	And where have you been working, Andy?
Andy:	In my brother's shop, upstairs. Is that against the law?
Inspector Atkinson:	No, not at all. What were you doing last night at two o'clock in the morning?
Andy:	Hmm, let me think … Surprise: I was in my bed, sleeping.
Inspector Atkinson:	Do you have any witnesses for that?
Andy:	No, I usually sleep alone.
Inspector Atkinson:	Do you know where Bold Street is?
Andy:	No, no idea.
Inspector Atkinson:	That's interesting … hmmm … do you know a man called Andrew MacAllister?
Andy:	Is he a bus driver?
Inspector Atkinson:	Yes, he is. What do you know about him?
Andy:	He drove the bus I usually take to the city centre, and he sometimes drank a beer at the same pub I go to, and he talked a lot to my girlfriend recently, especially while I was in prison. That's all.
Inspector Atkinson:	That's quite a lot. Thank you very much Andy. You are under arrest. I believe you murdered Andrew MacAllister last night in Bold Street.

Inhalt der Audio-CD

Track	Page	Unit, Exercise	Title
1	19	Unit 1, Ex 8	Holidays in Scotland
2	24	Unit 2, Ex 2	Hobbies
3	27	Unit 2, Ex 5	Families
4	35	Unit 3, Ex 2	Mr. and Mrs Smith come back home
5	40	Unit 3, Ex 5	Talk before the party
6	41	Unit 3, Ex 6	Party talk II
7	43	Unit 3, Ex 8	Talk after the party
8	45	Unit 3, Test, 3	Giving a party is not always fun!
9	80	Unit 6, Ex 8	At the computer club
10	93	Unit 7, Test, 1	Birthday presents
11	102	Unit 8, Ex 6	1. Helen and her friend
12	102	Unit 8, Ex 6	2. Helen and the doctor's office
13	103	Unit 8, Ex 8	1. What answering machines tell you
14	104	Unit 8, Ex 8	2. What you say to answering machines
15	105	Unit 8, Ex 8	3. What people say when they call back Call 1 Alice
16	105	Unit 8, Ex 8	3. What people say when they call back Call 2 The teacher
17	105	Unit 8, Ex 8	3. What people say when they call back Call 3 Andy
18	105	Unit 8, Ex 8	3. What people say when they call back Call 4 City Center Films
19	130	Unit 10, Ex 1	Check-up
20	132	Unit 10, Ex 2	A morning in inspector Atkinson's life
21	133	Unit 10, Ex 3	Inspector Atkinson and Mr. Mitchum
22	134	Unit 10, Ex 4	Mr. Maple, a witness
23	135	Unit 10, Ex 5	How to get to Killer Joe and Revolver Andy
24	136	Unit 10, Ex 6	Inspector Atkinson talks to Killer Joe
25	136	Unit 10, Ex 6	Inspector Atkinson talks to Revolver Andy

Register